I REACH OVER

Poems by Scott B. Shappell, M.D., Ph.D.

और

**Spiritual Correspondences
on ALS, Death, and Living**

with Sally F. Kilpatrick, Katy Rigler,
Simon Hayward, Ph.D., M. Scott Lucia, M.D.

Forward by Stanley H. Appel, M.D.

Hekaśa Books are available at quantity discounts with bulk purchase for educational, business, or sales promotional use.

For information, please contact:
Hekaśa Publishing
1920 Abrams Parkway, #400
Dallas, TX 75214-6218
Phone: 214-321-4158
Fax: 214-827-5292
Email: info@hekasa.com
www.hekasa.com

Cover image by: Wayne Rigler
Cover design by: Scott B. Shappell and Scott Baber
Interior design by: Scott Baber

ISBN: (13 digit) 978-0-9832293-0-8

For my family and friends,
especially Heidi, Sally, and Travis
for all their love and support
during the adjustment to "it"

For all ALS patients everywhere,
living as bravely as possible,
and for their supporters,
trying to treat them with dignity.

Acknowledgements

The author wishes to thank, with all my professional respect and personal heart, my partners, Dr. Thomas Mattison and Dr. Trae Mattison, for giving me as much time as needed to grieve, adjust, and strive for the spiritual strength needed during my life with ALS. I also admire their insightful support of the research role from my previous professional life to re-emerge with an altered spirit. No finer pathologists and human beings could anyone ever hope to work with or be friends with. God bless you as you push on with our dreams.

I wish to thank my good friend John Fulmer, the laboratory and molecular diagnostics division supervisor at Avero Diagnostics in Dallas, for keeping things going so smoothly, including by performing so well in our ongoing research projects. Similarly, I'd like to thank my long time good friend Wayne Rigler, our Vice President of Sales and Marketing, who along with John have kept me informed and involved in manners allowing for the hellish adjustment to ALS. These relationships have reflected wonderful qualities far exceeding their already staggering levels of professional competence. I'd like to thank all of the personnel at Avero Diagnostics, for their past and current daily efforts in making a world-class lab that focuses on people and service, helping to make a unique environment that was always a joy to be a part of. Thanks also for the support, love, and prayers.

I'd like to thank Wayne's wife, Katy, my dear, dear friend, who is amazingly intelligent, compassionate, and open-minded. In addition to the sincere heart-felt support that Wayne and Katy have given to Heidi and me since my ALS diagnosis, I'd like to specifically thank Katy for reviewing the poems, spiritual correspondences, and book reviews, as well as for providing the Introduction. Good and decent people seem to be the best way to meet other good and decent people. I met John Fulmer as a consequence of work-related interactions with his wife Amy and met Katy through Wayne. Likewise, through John and Amy, I recently met Scott Baber, whom I thank for doing such a great job on the book design and all the steps along the publishing process with Hekaśa Publishing.

I thank my Neurologist Dr. Daragh Heitzman and the incredible staff in his ALS clinic. There may not be a cure for ALS, but there's more to treating a patient than curing his or her disease. As with any terminal illness, along the way there is still the even more challenging aspect of taking care of the person, the human being, the spirit. As any "experienced" ALS patient knows, maintaining function as best as possible at all stages of decline is important to allow the crucial spiritual journey to proceed at all. I can't imagine a better group of individuals than the nursing, supervisory, PT, OT, respiratory therapy, medical equipment, social work and other staff of my ALS clinic at Texas Neurology. Bless you all (that's y'all or all y'all in TX) for the bravery to pleasantly confront this disease on a daily basis, and to develop emotionally challenging personal relationships with ALS patients and their families. Thanks to Dr. Heitzman even for some specific comments along the way that have contributed to enough of the "up moments" to undertake the psyche-taxing metaphorical steps, such as those presented in daily life and the compilation of this book. I also thank him for facilitating communication with his friend and colleague Dr. Stanley Appel.

I am so very grateful to Dr. Appel for taking the time out of his unbelievably busy schedule to write the Forward and for recognizing the struggle that it represents in coming to terms with the unavoidable realities of ALS. This knowledge has informed his daily activities for decades, and likely along with all his prior and current patients, colleagues, and trainees, I appreciate in the deepest places of human sincerity the intelligence, commitment, and compassion that he has uniquely displayed in a brilliant and inspiring clinical and research career that has included major focus on ALS.

Thanks so much to Dr. Simon Hayward and Dr. Scott Lucia for sharing their personal thoughts for this volume, as well as for their commitment to excellence in every aspect of past and ongoing research collaborations. It is a rare treasure indeed to be shown that even in the competitive and demanding world of biomedical research, there are those with not only brilliance and dedication, but with collegiality, integrity, and senses of humor. Thanks also for reminding me that the best aspects of mature souls can be appreciated and serve as a source of strength even when things change so drastically during our seemingly carefully planned careers and lives.

I give great thanks to my family for support, encouragement and unquestioned love, not only in the more immediate peri-diagnosis time frame with its surrealistic grimness, but the ongoing setting of never imagined physical and psychological adjustments. Thanks to my brother Steven and his wife Cindy for visiting us so early after April 21, 2009 and helping with the initial assault on the wine cellar and the blunt and sometimes painful, but necessary conversations in the initial phases of beginning to come to terms with things. Thanks to Heidi's Uncle John, Aunt Kathy, Cousins Heather and Jenny and Aunt Marcia, Uncle Ave, and Cousins Hilary and Emily for coming to visit and for sharing good food, good wine, and good conversation during the T-shirt commemorated "Farewell to Scott Shappell, The Physical Form 2010 Tour".

Thanks to my father-in-law Mike and mother-in-law Helen for everything over the past sixteen years: from accepting me and loving me immediately, being great "neighbors" when living 3 houses up the road in Nashville and being great co-diners when living a generous 2.5 miles away in Dallas, to the most recent times of helping with so many little things in our daily lives. Having you in my life has made loving your daughter an even richer experience.

Thanks to my mom and dad, Alice and Ralph Shappell, who have always shown the most amazingly humble love and care to all of their children at every stage of our lives. Without any worldly motives and as a reflection of God's love and grace, they imparted, along with a likely dose of genetic intelligence and a straight forward non-selfish work ethic, their non-severable support as well as daily lessons in treating all others with respect, fairness, and service. Even as they now approach the end of their own earthly journeys, they seem to have far less concern for their own fates than thoughts, prayers, and expressions of love for their son. I specifically thank my mom for enthusiastically allowing me to share "her" poem (*Ode to Mom*) by its inclusion in this volume.

I would like to express my love and deepest thanks to my sister Sally and her husband Kelsal for early visits after my ALS diagnosis, to participating in the RV trips we shared in the summer of 2009, to hosting me for six weeks in Colorado in the late spring of 2010, to shuttling me around and back and forth. I specifically thank Kel for all the wonderful meals and helpful tasks he continues to do as only a true brother would. I thank Sally for not only reading and commenting on poems, but for the time and support of sharing her insights and her love, as during the correspondences included in this book. This latest phase of our relationship builds upon a lifetime of closeness for which a dying human can truly be grateful for engaging in the human "game" to begin with. Thanks for listening to the evolving ideas coming from a possibly derailed mind and a hopefully growingly on-target soul, reading and discussing specific books, and for always giving me just what I seem to need to carry on.

Thanks to Baylor, Mox, and Brandy for adjusting so well to the growing impediments of canes, rollators, ramps and the paw-threatening terminator-like construction of the power-chair, while at the same time continuing to give us lessons in unconditional love.

As a brief surrogate of feelings that cannot be adequately expressed here or anywhere, I offer my deepest appreciation and love to my son Travis. I thank Travis for showing me that a dad with progressive motor weakness is still a real father. I thank him for picking me up when I fall physically and allowing me to help him when he stumbles as a young man progressively finding his own way. I thank and love him for believing in me no matter what I'm doing (whether medicine and science or writing poetry or a novel) and for the privilege of believing in him as he continually expands and expresses his intelligence and creativity.

And if my tears will allow me to continue, I thank my beautiful and brilliant wife Heidi from every level of what I have been and what I continue to become for showing me what true love really is. I thank you for being strong in the ways needed for dealing with all the objective aspects of wills and other personal planning, the necessary issues of clinic and equipment and home-modifications, and for communicating with friends and family about our condition (despite your own portion of this shared challenge). I also thank you for showing me, despite the reality of years, what commitment truly means in a relationship. For showing me that love evolves in the setting of physical life's unexpected detours and dead-ends and that love from and to the "inside" is forever empowering and rewarding and part of our souls' journey, my eternal gratitude is yours.

Foreword

When Scott Shappell asked me to write a Forward for this book, I was honored but disconsolate that he had been diagnosed with amyotrophic lateral sclerosis. We had only brief encounters when Scott underwent the rites of passage 20 years ago at Baylor College of Medicine, distinguishing himself as a brilliant MD/PhD graduate and then pursuing a successful career in translational research devoted to prostate cancer. Now he has ALS, a disease of motor neurons, one of the most challenging and frustrating disorders of mankind, and a daily battle that demands inner strength and courage, gradually and often inexorably compromising walking, lifting, speaking, swallowing and ultimately breathing. But ALS can also refocus one's priorities, lifting the human spirit and concentrating one's moral and emotional compass. One of our patients has actually insisted that he may have ALS but ALS doesn't have him; his family is grown and doing well, and now he can focus all his energy into helping others defeat ALS. And ALS has been transformational for Scott, shifting from a lifelong commitment to science and medicine to a spiritual flowering and awakening reflected in the inspirational poetry in this volume.

Over the last several decades I have been privileged to guide many patients in our Muscular Dystrophy Association-Amyotrophic Lateral Sclerosis Clinic at The Methodist Hospital in Houston, one of the first of many nationwide ALS clinics and Centers of Excellence sponsored by the MDA. Our clinic offers an opportunity for our multidisciplinary team to provide hope, and cutting-edge research is the best way to convey this hope. In patients, an expanding list of genetic mutations causes ALS in a minority of patients, but most cases likely result from the interaction of genetic and environmental triggers. In the last decade remarkable progress has been made in basic research, identifying multiple pathways that compromise motor neuron function. Yet translation of these exciting advances into meaningful therapy is not presently available and remains for the future. Nevertheless patients in our MDA/ALS multidisciplinary clinics are living longer with more quality by our focus on maintaining mobility, avoiding falls, maintaining nutrition, avoiding aspiration, and enhancing breathing functions with non-invasive ventilation.

Guiding our ALS patients has been a humbling and awe-inspiring experience made all the more meaningful by the deep well of courage that fuels their daily actions; their inner strength, dignity, and courage are continuous sources of inspiration. For the family, ALS is a test of caring and patience. For the physician it is a challenge to make a difference. Yet when ALS patients lose their neuromuscular function, their response is unique; they become all heart and spirit. They are "nice guys" focused on helping others, and that spirit is motivational for all of us concerned with patient care; and Scott Shappell is the personification of the "nice guy" committed to helping other ALS patients through the comforting message of his poetry.

Best regards,

Stan
Stanley H. Appel MD
Edwards Distinguished Endowed Chair for ALS
Director, Methodist Neurological Institute
Chair, Department of Neurology
Houston, TX

Table of Contents

Introduction

I met Scott and Heidi (Scott's wife) on December 12, 2003. It may seem odd that I remember the exact date that I met them, especially because Scott, Heidi, and I did not become fast friends that night. In fact, it would be several more years before I would become *real* friends with Scott and Heidi in the sense that my husband, Wayne, had always anticipated. Wayne and Scott worked at the same company and the night we met was their company Christmas party. Scott had recently come to work there while my husband had been there a few years, but the two of them had become good friends in a short period of time. Wayne was looking forward to introducing me to Scott and Heidi, as he knew we would hit it off. He explained that Heidi was, not unlike myself, an independent, intelligent, and compassionate woman. She and Scott were "thinkers" and he had visions of the four of us becoming companions.

I had been to enough of Wayne's company's Christmas parties to know that I probably wasn't going to have a good time, but it was necessary for us to make an appearance. I was pregnant with our third child and just days before the party I had begun cramping. My doctor ran several labs and found that my hormones were very low; she felt sure that I was going to miscarry. Since it was early in the pregnancy she had advised me to take it easy and not lift anything, but to go to the party. I was devastated, but I was determined she was wrong and that the baby would be fine. I remember the date because it was one of the worst days of my life, and strangely enough, Scott and Heidi unknowingly provided me some saving grace that evening.

Scott and Heidi came to the party, but their appearance was just that – an appearance. Wayne made a quick introduction and the two of them scooted out almost as soon as they had arrived. They were pleasant, and I had the feeling that Wayne was right, I would enjoy their company, but it was not to be that night. Shortly after they left I began to miscarry. It was emotionally much harder than I ever could have imagined. I did not want to go back to the party. I wanted to curl into a ball and cry. Wayne was waiting for me as I came out of the bathroom and I told him I wanted to go. This was more difficult than it seemed as Wayne's employer always depended on Wayne to close down the party. However, Scott and Heidi had already made their exit so they had unknowingly removed the pressure on us to stay. I was grateful. That was the last time I saw Scott and Heidi for several years.

Little did I know that four years later we would all be living in a different state and Wayne and Scott would be working for a completely different company before we would really get to know each other. Although I kept up with their lives and they knew of mine through Wayne, I did not see Scott and Heidi again on a social basis until Wayne took a job in another state with Scott in 2007. In the meantime I had had another child, suffered a serious medical complication from a routine surgery and moved away from my "home" in beautiful Tennessee to the strange, hot, and flat area of concrete, otherwise known as Dallas. Things had certainly changed.

However, this time when I met Scott and Heidi, they already seemed like old friends. Perhaps it was the move and the desperate ache for companionship in a strange land. Perhaps it was the struggle with my medical condition and the plethora of knowledge Scott and Heidi, being physicians, jointly held regarding my medical condition. Perhaps it was our shared knowledge of my "home" in Tennessee that made them so comfortable. Maybe it was our shared love of books that was discovered when we visited their home. Perhaps it was the interesting way the Spirit moves to bring people into our lives exactly when we need them most. I choose to believe it was the Spirit bringing kindred souls together to create something none of us could ever have imagined.

In early 2009 Wayne began coming home from work complaining that Scott was "not himself". Scott had always been a night person and it was not uncommon for Wayne to receive work emails from him well into the wee hours of the morning, but lately he had been working more and more even into the early dawn hours and then not showing up to the office until it was almost quitting time for everyone else. Scott and Wayne hardly saw each other anymore. Wayne said Scott seemed "on edge" and even "defensive". Wayne was worried. I believe it was April of that year that we discovered the reason why – Scott was diagnosed with ALS, also known as Lou Gehrig's disease.

I immediately knew what Scott was going to be dealing with in the very near future. My first college degree was in physical therapy and I was very familiar with the disease. ALS typically affects men, Scott was the right age for symptoms to manifest, and he is one of the most intelligent people I have ever known (ALS typically affects people with a well above average intelligence). The muscle weakness he had been experiencing in his leg was not a pinched nerve as he had first hoped for, but the result of the nerve cells innervating his leg slowly dying. The worst part was, it was going to get worse, much worse, and it was going to eventually affect all of his muscles, including those used for swallowing and breathing (the failure of which is the most common cause of death for ALS patients). I knew his life expectancy was not good, the average being 2 to 5 years. As I told Wayne about the disease, we wept for Scott and Heidi.

Understandably, Scott began to close himself off from the mundane tasks of everyday life (including in his position as Medical Director of his laboratory). Weeks went by when they did not hear from him at work. I remember Heidi commenting that days would go by when he wouldn't get out of bed. Scott had always been a workaholic. He was a searcher, and prior to his diagnosis, Scott's search for meaning and knowledge is what drove his scientific career. It wasn't just that he loved work; it was that he wanted to know more, to learn more, to discover all of the things that were hidden. At first, many of Scott's friends thought they saw him giving up on everything that had meaning for him and worried that he had resigned from life. However, it soon became apparent that was not the case at all.

When Scott was diagnosed with ALS his search simply shifted. While science was still important to him, he innately knew that work would not provide the answers he needed. Strangely enough, while Scott was closing himself off from ordinary things, an extraordinary window opened in his life. He remembered the poetry and metaphysics he had been interested in during his younger years. He felt drawn to study them again. All of his adult years Scott had been searching outside of himself for meaning, knowledge, and purpose. After his diagnosis, Scott's quest did not end; instead, it innately turned inward. Scott and I began to have long and exciting discussions about books, the Divine, and life's purposes. Scott knew I was a Presbyterian minister and that I had also studied in the Graduate Department of Religion at Vanderbilt University. His interests in science, metaphysics, mysticism, and the Divine coincided with many of the things I had studied and read.

Scott is still what many of us would consider to be a workaholic. Once he decides to do something, he does not rest until his task is completed. I have been amazed at his attention to detail and the thoroughness with which he studies. His passion for learning is evident in every comment, every footnote, and every email he sends. He has literally consumed entire books and volumes of poetry. His journey inward has become his work. This is not to say that it has not been difficult. I think if given the choice, Scott would trade in his diagnosis at any given moment for some semblance of life pre-ALS. However, Scott is thankful for his journey. His eyes are wide open as he looks at what the future holds, and for the first time in his adult life, he is able to see. I am thankful that he has chosen to share his vision with me.

I was privileged to read most of these poems as a near complete collection, intended for this current volume, and then receive for reading the remaining individual poems as the included collection was being assembled. As a fan and experienced reader of poetry, I was impressed by the quality of Scott's poems. I was even more struck by the nature of the powerful emotions expressed, a complete and utter opening up by a soul undergoing a tremendously difficult journey.

I love the title he chose for this book, *I Reach Over*. It is so full of meaning. Reaching implies effort, not a simple leaning, but a real effort to acquire something that is not easily attained. The title also holds the implication that there is something more to behold than what is evident in our lives. There is movement in the poems. Movement is not something that is simply physical; movement is also growth, strength, resilience, and bearing the weight of heartache. In my responses to Scott following my reading of these poems, I frequently made comments regarding specific poems, thoughts invoked by the overall aura of a poem or on specific lines and stanzas that I found particularly meaningful and strong.

Darkness?, the first poem in this volume, and the second poem to be written by Scott in this current life era, is very powerful and mystical. I love all of the "people" making an appearance in the darkness of this poem. The author has always been a "night person", as my husband can attest. Work related emails from Scott were not uncommonly sent between 1:00 and 4:00 in the morning. With Wayne being more of a morning person, lab related details were thus not uncommonly "discussed" (at least electronically) close to 24 hours a day. As expressed in Scott's poem, night (darkness) is not a time to be afraid. It is a time to be in awe and wonder. The last line, "Awakened by the magic darkness" highlights this sentiment. Darkness isn't all we thought it was. After all, weren't we all born from a void and nested in a pitch-black womb…the same darkness we found comforting and necessary.

In *Interrogation of a Retrovirus*, the second poem in the volume, we see a common element in this series of Scott's poems: the collision of science and strong sentiment. I like the things that are juxtaposed in this poem. The author is angry, and yet still searching for meaning and purpose in the situation causing these burning emotions. Although targeted at the virus causing HIV in this particular poem, this theme becomes expanded in the poet's personal encounter with ALS, and consequently, with the universal situation of death. I have also been fortunate to read Scott's recently completed first novel, which deals in part with HIV and particularly neurological complications of HIV and AIDS. Strong compassion presented as an occasional element within a broader range of humanity is subtly explored. In the poem, we see in the background of a terrible virus, the suggestion that humans are the guilty party of some of the more negative social aspects of this horrific disease. I found the second stanza to contain particularly great lines raising these considerations (that humans faced with this epidemic are the lesser of the evolved parties of the disease process):

> *Laying quiet like an evil temptress*
> *for many years until you rise to rob me*
> *of my youth, my energy, and my dignity,*
> *as the ignorance of my less evolved species*
> *doesn't see you as you really are. And*
> *only sees me, an easy projection of their fear.*

In the last stanza of *Ode to Ganesh*, the third poem in the current volume, the poet realizes that the spiritual journey "inflicted" upon him by his illness is indeed perhaps an "unexpected blessing", something proclaimed in the first line of the poem. By writing to Lord Ganesh, the God commonly invoked by writers, the poet acknowledges that he indeed has a new purpose, one worth living for: to write.

Scott seems to put a lot of thought into the titles of his poems. They are often provocative, brief phrases summarizing or supplementing the sentiment of the poem, rather than just the first or another phrase from the body of the poem. *Ghosts of Ourselves Present* is a good example, and *Strands* is a powerful illustration of how the title, even so brief, can cast a rich psychological setting to the concepts explored in the poem. The theme of current human disconnection is explored again in the social satire of *"I'm Having a Mocha Latte and Driving to Work"*. I really liked this poem, as so many times I want to connect to others in ways that seem almost impossible. The "stuff" of our lives often gets in the way of really connecting with other people on a deep and meaningful level. People look at me funny when I say I don't want "stuff" anymore. Scott's last line of this poem summed up for me why I say such things: "I say them for my '*soul's sake*.'"

Other poems in the first section of the current volume (*Observations and Reflections*) touch in very specific contexts on themes greatly expanded on in the latter sections of the poetry (*Moving Within and Upward*). For example, in *Pearl Harbor Day in Big Bend National Park* (appropriately written on December 7th), I do note a "yes, often times and unfortunately" response to the author's question: *Is the blindness of nationalism greater than human care?* This poem, again, explores the struggle between science and humanity, an ongoing difficulty the poet speculates on from the perspective of an experienced and accomplished scientist. And in *On Reading Gide's "Immoralist,"* we again see that the poet has been led by his personal journey to a place encountering both wisdom and faith, where the Jungian concept of God as both good and evil is explored against the background of the novel.

However, it is particularly in the strikingly haunting "dark poems" that the poet rips himself open with the shock and horror of his new physical state and his having to come to terms with his paralyzing and terminal condition of ALS. *Incurable Blues* is so honest and real. I was and am still amazed that Scott put these feelings down on paper. However, I am glad that he put it in print. It needs to be said...and read. So often we keep these feelings inside thinking them too ugly, too difficult to share. Scott goes out on a limb here by writing them down, as things always seem more real once we say (or write) them. Once we let the feelings we have take on words, they no longer have a hold on us; instead they take on a "life" of their own as readers interpret and re-interpret them within the context of their own lives time and time again. I am sure Scott was confronting his Demons when writing this poem. I know I was when I read it. As stated in the overwhelmingly powerful last two lines of the poem *Present Awareness*:

Only the journey into the depths from where there is no coming back
Is the sole thing truly human; the single thing we all will share

Social critique is again visited in the *Darkness* section, as in the incrimination of society and the educational system in *Formula*. As a parent who has decided to home school my children, I particularly appreciate the possible danger that an overly rigid, "brain-washing" system can prevent the open minds needed to see the greater aspects of humanity that Scott searches for in these collected poems. From the last two lines of *Formula*:

> *Appears you never saw the inner light for deviation*
> *Took all the wrong turns to make the straight line nowhere*

No one can go through the process that Scott, other ALS patients, and those facing other serious illnesses have to encounter without the love and support of family and friends. There will be moments of utter aloneness that individuals will journey through in solitude. But the strength to encounter these and to emerge on the other side is so often gathered not only by a personal spirituality, but also through the bolstering presence of one's support group. Despite the darkness and personal suffering conveyed in some of these poems, the author's recognition and appreciation of the loved ones in his life is beautifully conveyed in the poems contained within the *Relationships* section of the book.

I cried through this entire section. However, I also smiled and laughed. These poems are very touching...and so very real to me, especially after having met many of the people whom they are about. I thank Scott for sharing them with me, and now with all of us. Many times we don't tell the people who mean so much to us in our lives how important they really are. We forget that they need to hear us say "thank you," and "I love you." I suspect that these particular poems were the toughest to write, and yet the most fulfilling for me to read. They truly nourished my soul.

The "feminine" qualities of wisdom, also touched upon in other poems, are incorporated into the religious subjects of direct relevance to the poet's sister Sally's Christian educational mission in the "Walk to Emmaus", which is celebrated in the poem *To Serve*.

> *The wisdom of Sophia guided His hand.*
> *Only a virgin, like Nature un-sacked*
> *could give all Her Children of Man*
> *the Son who would lead the way back.*

These topics were encountered by the author in some of his readings of Jung (See Book List at end). In this poem, the poet feels the loss of the feminine and wisdom aspects of mankind. These feelings parallel some of the poet's other realizations of deficiencies in humanity. We may have the opportunity to revisit these and related ideas in a rumored second volume of Scott Shappell's poetry.

Scott's *Ode to Mom* included herein is a very moving poem. I had the privilege of meeting Scott's mother, Alice, on one occasion. She is, indeed, a wonderful woman. I can only hope that one day my children will feel the same about me as Scott does about her. I know that Scott's mother and I will cherish this poem always.

How appropriate that the first poem written by the author following his diagnosis and stepping back somewhat from his medical scientist career was *I Reach Over*. This poem was written for Scott's wife, Heidi, and reflects their relationship, including how it must inevitably evolve as the poet proceeds to his probable unnaturally early death. There is so much meaning to the poem, and to the title, from which this entire collection so rightly takes its name. As I read this poem, I cried…and smiled…and cried. How lucky Scott is.

There is function in the form and I love the flow of the sections of poetry as assembled by the poet. I think the poems are grouped perfectly and poetically in themselves. The poem *Words and Blankets,* with which the section *Moving Within and Upward* leads off, shows us the movement taking place in the form. The poet addresses the reality of the physical aspects of his ALS in a fundamentally mortal and existential way:

> *I don't like to be completely covered;*
> *I get warm, I need some air to pass over me,*
> *To bring me movement, to know that I'm alive*

And in the next lines, he powerfully compares this physical impairment and survival urge to the process of the primal survival of a shark (an interesting metaphor in its own right) that is maintained by the forces of nature:

> *To feed me like a moving shark who only rarely comes*
> *Completely still, not by choice but maybe fate,*
> *An inner knowledge that nature moves the ocean currents*

The inner knowledge written about in this poem refers to the poet's past, which gave him a vast arsenal of such in many areas, including feelings of dedication and compassion that arises from a career in medicine and insight into the natural physical world from a lifetime of scientific training. However, the poet's ongoing quest for inner knowledge has undergone a major directional and focus change, with a reawakened spiritual craving since his diagnosis. That shift is brilliantly portrayed in the structurally interesting poem *Ouch and Love*. This poem, in a seeming dialogue with the divine, portrays the feelings of despair encountered with the realization of the poet's new condition:

> *Why then have my little cells*
> *Died before their rightful season?*
> (from stanza V)

and:

I can't win, you're too big, so I engage
(from stanza VI)

The poem continues and also demonstrates the poet's awareness of an evolving spirit of rebirth:

Part of ever wholeness,
Even if not seen.
We move on, preach
The Word, You
Peace, dove,
Love!
(from last stanza)

As identified in some of the notes accompanying specific poems, a descent (or maybe an ascent?) to insanity (or maybe an enlightened spiritual state resembling a process easily confused with insanity) was an at least temporary mental status target for the poet's encounter against his grim disease enemy. We may never know how closely Scott came to approaching this target, or if he got there, how long he stayed. Anyone who knew him, even before his being diagnosed with ALS, knows that his high level of mental function often seemed otherworldly. All of this is to say, given his newfound quest superimposed on his pre-existing state, it comes as no surprise that the highly unconventional way of seeing things at least fully surfaced in some of Scott's poems. Nowhere is this as evident than in the poem *Outsiders Heading To The Grass* (see also poet's notes at end of book). I really like this poem! It is very deep, and I particularly love the imagery and mix of science and cynicism. As I had communicated to Scott during my reading of his poems, his use of imagery is particularly strong, but even more so in this poem. Likewise, from the very opening line, "*It was the winter of my Prozac solstice,*" I absolutely loved the poem *Dance*. Staggeringly imaginative lines are common to Scott's poems, and a few standouts are particularly noted here: *All the gray holiday dust….transparent protective soul paste…*

Interestingly, Dante's *Divine Comedy* resurfaced in both our lives during this time. I presented it as a book for my children to read and study in their home schooling curriculum, and Scott revisited it during his extensive readings on his Spiritual Journey (See Book List), as he wanted to read poet Robert Pinsky's translation of the *Inferno*. Therefore when the symbolic Beatrice shows up at the end of this sensational poem, *Dance*, it was all the more meaningful to me. In this poem the poet personally begins to recognize that he is more than his disease, more than a gradually dwindling physical capability:

Beatrice laughed a gentle tug of last minute solace, saying:
"Silly poet, don't you know yet
That we dance with our souls and not our legs"

These last lines in particular demonstrate the author's shifting attitude regarding his journey since his diagnosis. Scott wrote this poem on New Year's Eve/New Years Day, and I noted to him that his poems were just getting better and better. *Dance* is movement and readers can sense the movement that has taken place in the poet's life up to that time; the movement the poet discovers defies his growing paralysis.

The subsequent poem in this collection, *Divine Slap in the Face*, written in essence to reflect a correspondence between the poet and an initially perceived uncompassionate God is as blunt an expression of anger and frustration as can possibly be expressed. ALS patients are likely to be able to particularly relate, for example, given the allusion to aspects of being "mechanical" (reflecting perhaps the gradual accumulation of medical assist devices to try and maintain as much function as possible). Referring to God as a "*Dark Lord,*" "*Mother Fucker,*" and "*Pseudo God of hopeful lives with no real hope,*" this poem reaches down to a most raw anger and utter despair. This poem made Scott a little uncomfortable after he wrote and shared it. He somewhat sarcastically commented to his sister that he "may be going to hell for this one." Sally reassured him that it is not only okay, but also fully appropriate to feel this way. This dialogue between Scott and Sally is included in the wonderful section of personal spiritual correspondences between the poet and his sister in a separate section following the poems themselves. The poet does not dwell in his anger, as expected for poems in a *Moving Inward and Upward* section; the poet finds room for hope, as reflected in the message he includes from the deity he has been bitterly yelling at:

And still you fight instead of love. I like your angry spirit, but it is time to channel it
To what you should have always realized: you think, you love, you marvel, you're blessed

And in the last stanza, of special relevance to patients facing a premature PHYSICAL demise, and who may be also feeling sensitive towards their weakness, and the growing metal and plastic supports to their daily function, the deity continues:

You are immortal. You are not canned goods. ...

And in the poignant last line, somewhat similar to the conclusion of *Dance:*

9

Why do you think that a wheel chair made by caring men is any different than your finite legs?

This poem also illustrates the learning curve the poet finds himself on, and he hopes that sharing his journey will help other people with ALS (and other debilitating diseases) realize they are not alone. However, this poem speaks on a deeper level than even Scott may be aware because it tells of a prematurely forced path that ultimately we all, as mortal humans, will find ourselves encountering in one fashion or another during our lifetimes. Forced growth, whether resulting from a physiological disease or dis-ease with our lives in general is always accompanied by growing pains.

One day later the poet composed the poem *She*, which follows *Divine Slap in the Face* in the current volume. As conveyed at the time of my original reading, I like that this poem comes after the last one. It makes sense that way. The journey continues. The next poem is somewhat unique in the collection, being composed in large part in frank dialogue form. *The Assassination of Physics by the Unknown Aqua Man* is very Hafiz-like. Hafiz, the Sufi poet who includes reference to himself in his great poems, has been a source of inspiration to me. I was privileged to give a large collection of his divinely inspired poetry to Scott for Christmas 2009, and particularly pleased to learn of his enjoyment of these love-infused poems and to see the hint of a Hafiz-like dialogue showing up in this particular poem. Scott's prior studying of physics before his embarking on medical science education and practice and his return to philosophical issues raised by modern physics are reflected in part by the content of the debate of a physicist and a God-man (perhaps Krishna himself) in this highly creative poem. I love the mystical quality and the story aspect of it.

Following his sharing of the first 31 or so of the poems of this collection with me in one large bolus and the evolution of the idea to publish these poems in a format accompanied by other book portions targeted in particular to issues related to his personal experience with ALS, Scott subsequently presented to me the remaining poems for my reading and thoughts. These poems are largely contained in the section *Moving Within and Upward, Part II*. Some short, sparse poems of breathtakingly gentle fragility are included here. I really like the poem *Collapsing. Conversion Order*, the longest poem within this collection is a story/parable style poem, which I also really like. Again, the style of it reminds me very much of Rumi or Hafiz. I very much love the imagery (an increasingly characteristic quality of a Scott Shappell poem) and its descriptiveness. I also enjoyed *Remote*. The idea of a nun in a bikini contest not only demonstrates the utter dissolution of social and psychological barriers emerging in Scott's poetry, but remains a subtle illustration of the sense of humor he has retained, a quality, that for those who know him, is as dominant an aspect of his personality as any other. May that never depart. His perpetual sense of humor, his ability to make others laugh, and the balance of his utterly undeterred determination in all aspects of his work and life by the ability to laugh and joke are a constant source of fresh air that we are glad to see increasingly return as he progresses in the adjustment to his illness. That and a degree of bluntness (sexual and otherwise), which can be rather shocking to the uninitiated (and sometimes even to the familiar), are qualities that we celebrate daily in this medicine man and newly awakened poet.

Upon reading these last few poems to be included in this volume, I had decided that the sparse and utterly heartfelt *Ice* was my favorite poem. However, upon reading *Essence*, such a powerful poem, I decided that perhaps I had two favorites.

Although the creation of these poems, and the hopefully many others that follow, may have been immediately prompted by the author's experience in being diagnosed with ALS and coming to grips with the psychological and personal aspects of this terrible disease, the poems indeed stand on their own merit. Because of the powerful emotional content, some of the poems are very difficult to read. As I read them, I imagined the courage required to scream these things, cry these words, and finally embrace oneself. Scott has truly given me, and everyone who reads this volume, a gift: truly the ultimate gift of his Self by allowing me (and us) the privilege of "feeling" Scott's soul. For this, I give him my deepest and sincerest thanks.

I believe a new voice of poetry exists in the United States. I thank Scott so much for sharing these poems with me. I cannot lie: some of them were quite intense, to the point that I began to wonder why I agreed to read them. However, after a couple of glasses of wine and a box of tissues, I was feeling so privileged that he chose to share these with me. I did indeed feel "glimpses of the Soul", not only the poet's, but mine, too, as well as something bigger. I have laughed, cried, smiled, curled into a ball, and danced with joy as I read these poems. And that may be the gift a true poet gives: movement. I cannot wait to see the book. It will be one that never gets shelved, one that will remain on my nightstand (where only the good ones are) to remind me to live, to feel, to think, to cherish, to love, and to cry...and to curse like a sailor every now and then, too. After all, that is part of living. All I can say to Scott is: Thank you! Thank you! Thank you!

Katy Rigler
May 2010

OBSERVATIONS
AND
REFLECTIONS

Darkness?

Night oozes its primordial juices
through the invisible veins of walls.
Pluto shines cerebral radium along
a breeze through open windows.
Sirens wale, near and far. Cats shriek
their random alley insemination.
Lovers snore in putrid armpits.

And it rises, from grass in parks.
It ascends in booths of all night diners.
It grows from the spine of ancient letters.
It climaxes from the desk
chair of the reclusive insomniac,
riding waves of music metaphors.
Pencils quiver in hidden resonance.

Jehovah sleeps in luxurious robes.
Allah tosses and turns in slumber.
Even Jesus and his cousin Krishna
nod in empty plastic chairs
of laundromats and taxi cabs.
In the world of clocks and schedules,
stockbrokers sleep martini comas.

And it grows, from the bars
to eggs and coffee of the liberated.
It manifests densely, in elongating
ash of the loosely held cigarette.
It ruptures from the fiery eyes
of the restless manic unknowns.
It gushes red from exploding hearts.

This is Galileo's orbiting time,
Poe's immortal span of perfect somber.
The blind close their naïve eyes.
Dreams descend they may absorb.
Tomorrow they compartmentalize the gray,
But spirits walk among us when
all the concrete rules are gone.

And Escher's birds fly East and West.
Directions, like the sun, are meaningless.
At night we know both black and white
and colors come from inner guides.
We hear them drifting in the
recesses of the limbic mesh.
Awakened by the magic darkness.

(ss 10/01/2009)

Interrogation of a Retrovirus

Sneaky little fucker, so small; only seen
by instruments we don't carry to the bars.
Leaking through my love, my sex, my needs;
Using your evolution to bind to parts of me
I never knew, or appreciated.
Why did you come when he came?

Laying quiet like an evil temptress
for many years until you rise to rob me
of my youth, my energy, and my dignity,
as the ignorance of my less evolved species
doesn't see you as you really are. And
only sees me, an easy projection of their fear.

Why weren't you happy in your quiet
home of the starving, poor, and innocent
disease ridden mystery people?
Why did you come to our land, the home
of cocaine, fast cars, and leather,
all of man's greatest accomplishments?

Why did you have to mix your pesky
little life with our precious seed?
Why did you rob the already robbed?
Why did you poison the blood
of the hopeless and confused?
Why steal the freedom from the different?

My glands swell and then they die.
My friends, my lovers, they all perish.
You show no mercy, just kill efficiently.
Will we ever learn to co-exist?
The smart lab monkeys love you,
because of you, so many jobs.

So many broken peoples in so many lands.
You bring fascination and suffering never known.
You make us smarter, you make us sadder.
You mutate and move on, as if you didn't care.
You are driven by forces we don't understand,
Just like the people whose lives you've ruined.

(ss 10/08/2009)

Ode to Ganesh

What an unexpected blessing, inspiration yours
Encountered in the nature of that spirit whose guitar
Did bridge the East meets West, our guru Dark Horse:
Gentle, dying young, delivered chants beside the sitar.
I bathe in Hindu waters, breathe in Vedic ethers,
And discover you there, wisdom guide of writers.

You welcome the determined spirit of the messenger.
You gently calm the restless mind of the distracted.
In my case, you push aside my impending horror
And let my humble words rise from incense ashes.
My Lord, you grace me with a drive and purpose:
One last season of nobility in a life past glorious.

Where rested your loving head, cut off by the great Cobra?
Jealous husband, evenness of gods shown by manly deeds.
How sad to lose your crown divine, sliced by God your Father,
And gain instead the circus trunk and ears of Disney movies.
And riding on a rat? Most New World movers and doers
Would cringe at the urban pest of New York sewers.

But I have known the elephants, the great "beasts".
They have blocked the roads of our open Rovers.
We watched them graciously lumber in the reeds
And play their dance in the Okavango Delta waters.
One of your kind came to my deck which upon I wrote,
Not bothering me or the baboons on top our neighbors' hut.

I have sat side by side with your giant earthly kin
While others shrieked and noted the proximity
I finished the last page of a masterpiece from Boyd's able pen
Knowing from your lack of mal-intent that I could peacefully.
As your goad serves to drive my soul from all the fake around me,
Nature, ultimate mahout, steered your comrade my heart to see.

You, round bellied guardian of temple entryway
Who wears the sign of Shiva around your happy middle,
You are steady under all duress and never sway.
Leader of the ganas, now guide me as I travel just a little
More in this life; your pasam to destroy the clueless "I"
Carried for way too long. Blessed Lord of journeys nigh.

(ss 11/10/2009)

Ghosts of Ourselves Present

Little Johnnie made straight A's.
Little Suzie took piano lessons.
They both grew up to be perfect specimens
of self-preserving politicians.

John and all his twins were MBAs.
Sue married one and served in PTAs.
They each produced their two point two children
And raised them with kits from catalogues.

John and Sue stumbled on each other
In the magic late night wires of the web
California to New York was not unclear
To say things they really couldn't speak or hear.

One day Jonathan looked around to nothing.
He wrote a note of emptiness to wife and kids.
He drove out to a cul-de-sac in Middledom
And spewed his brains into the station wagon.

Susan found she'd one less bud.
She poured a scotch and checked the kids.
She resumed her quest for late night Quan,
Chatted into emptiness to find another John.

(ss 10/06/2009)

Pearl Harbor Day in Big Bend National Park

American Flag hanging at half-mast
Entering that celebration of Nature vast
La Gran Curva, borderland of enemies old
Northern Chihuahuan Desert, past dwelling of the bold

Warm here today, maybe like that December hour
Sun and youth mixed in innocence at Pearl Harbor
When the Emperor's Zeroes came down like red-tailed hawks
Their torpedoes like irreversible talons of future dark

Wasn't there enough beach for everyone?
I have been to Oahu, the sand goes on and on.
Surely an Island nation had much its own share,
Is the blindness of nationalism greater than human care?

What can Nature teach us today of all days?
The lava peaks project their faces skyways
Like the masts of battleships at our western furthest
Igneous rocks formed from a heat below the earth's surface

Ships for war, to flex our growing might
Sunk in a moment, bring the sleeping Giant to the fight
But the great rocks we see were formed long ago
No moment or ages can erode, they persist to show us how

Bodies and ships lay at the bottom of the harbor
Left and horror stacked as testament to anger
Unlike sedimentary rock around us, limestone from older waters
Of ancient millennia, skeletons of past sea animals

Graveyard rocks formed under gentle, natural time
Weren't there enough mountains for all to marvel and to climb?
Nature's chemistry is everywhere we look and go:
In balance; not like the alchemy in fire bombing Tokyo

Modern physics has shown beyond all doubt
That we, like the lion, wolf, and javelina stout
Are all the same, divine energy in mountain, man, and fauna
Sadly, the same physics that would annihilate Hiroshima

In this great park, where today we honor pain
We notice more the peace of all that dies and lives again
In the midst of desert, flowers burst from the prickly pear
We have enough Her bounty to not tarnish, but to share

(ss 12/7/2009)

Strands

The dust and tumbleweed of golden hair at the corner of the room
The sleeping, twitching dog on the sofa who wakes each time you speak
The blunted grass in cracks within the sidewalk as you walk your neighborhood
The smooth leather seats of your fancy car that hold you during your work week

A bum sleeps soundly with a rumbling belly as you pass under a bridge
A closer look would show tobacco stains on his fingers and crumbling teeth
A group of teenage girls drinking lattes with cell phone face appendages
A coffee shop with closely spaced strangers, a Lap Top a piece

The men who put your walls up and your hardwoods down
The lady from whom your dog derived; the woman who helped pick color schemes
The long dead man who poured the concrete of your older part of town
The factory worker who installed your auto seats, his family, and his dreams

A mother who may once have harbored higher hopes for her homeless son
A complex societal machine that takes crops to cigarettes to stores
A thousand workers in other lands give us beans and hand-helds with our family plans
Another thousand that we'll never know make our little screens and silent keyboards

(ss 12/12/2009)

On Reading Gide's *Immoralist*

Keats I'll never be, but long ago I did read Homer and Shakespeare
All The Iliad, though I may have skipped some in the list of ships
Almost every page of The Odyssey, thrilling return to Penelope dear
The tragedies ripped my heart even if words felt weird from out my lips

But Greco-Roman tunnel vision does not display all of the world
And English literature soaked Western lore only starts to pry the eyes
Pious man makes his angry God the perfect good we strive toward
Evil urges that must be buried, surely from another source arise

But to blame Satan is to oversimplify the "rules" that guide our being
I have looked to the dark and seen a real man struggle with urges human
Gide's Michel did as he must to truly be; TB like Keats killed Marceline
Lust for boys is but one urge within the mortal conscious spectrum

The God I recognized in Bollingen's dark towers is harsh as well as kind
Only if man sees at last his same full self can he make life's hard decisions
Falling short of mythical divine can only come if he to instinct blind
In a world that doesn't always map to just right and wrong directions

I have looked to the East and believe that God is everything and all
Deeds good or bad are just actions by men with or without the lights turned on
Act towards others as they, like you, just droplets from the grand dispersal
Don't invoke a pitchfork wielding fallen Angel for lack of your Self recognition

(ss 12/17/2009)

La Bella Luna

(for LRD's Bella, whose tongue I've had in my mouth far too many times)

In the agave scented dusty alleyway
The cold-footed mistress of the cult mischievous
Holds court as palm leaves in arid winds sway
In another life, another time, she was a much feared countess

She wore a black turtleneck and tilted beret
A cigarette of impassioned revolutionary sentiment
Dangled granite ash in the dark side of the café
Her restless ass twitched as fiery reinforcement

As tango dancers sweated in each other's embrace
Upstairs, to a rhythm of happy ignorance
The impish plans for the Mexican race
Unfolded from her sharp teeth and leaping countenance

But that was a former life, a long time ago
It was the age of passion, the age of righteous sin
Before NAFTA, before the side-striped El Camino
When spirited women steered the testicles of men

Now in the gentler techno age, in six pound form
She silently leads the double top-secret mongrel plan
Her squinty eyes belie the intent of devious swarm
Pooping on the floor the least our worries from this canine clan

(ss 01/07/2009)

"I'm Having a Mocha Latte and Driving to Work"

Close your eyes, log in your mind
Forget the silly Maya that daily dims
The space round the coffee-pot grind
Plug into the heart which flows over craving brims

If the only human book you read
Is held on your lap or within your hand
And starts with Face, don't feel the need
To chronicle your diet, shits, mundane thoughts du jour

Twitter Dee, Twitter Dumb; give me more
The Collective Consciousness is now server based
If all men can speak, let your voices soar
Ask for truth, seek forever, digitally paced

Video killed radio; trips to the rental place
Killed the ozone; IMs killed the handshake
First time ever for the talking monkey race,
We can all connect: Do it for your soul's sake

(ss 01/04/2010)

Femme Animale

Mist ascends off the manhole covers
Climbs up unseen channels from the core
Spreads out like the fog of ancient swamps
Over the glistening moist cobble stones
Of the posher downtown streets nostalgic
For the shoes of horses pulling carriages
Of the slightly over dressed naughty nobility

Conspiring rays from the ritualistic
Lustful streetlamps pierce the darkness
Reflecting off sparsely scattered puddles
To cast ascending sparks on the fashion hose
Of a toned and shapely calf descending into
The leather of a spike-healed designer boot
Spraying animal must within the radius of eager steps

Inside a club protected always from the sun
Where the cult of midnight gathers all to purge
The numbness of society by melting
Into the damp Earth once again
Lost and found, she offers up her organs
And immerses the rhythms of her gyrations
Into the savage beat, the raving temple roar

The sweat gifted on the dance floor
Is of a different Nature than that expressed
From the racquetball court or extracted
In nervous boardroom presentations
More primal. It dries to a pheromonal luster
In the cool electric dawn, waiting for a cab
It can work its magic if called for by the Gods

(ss 04/17/2010)

Darkness

Incurable Blues

"Despair upon despair", an agitation from the deepest wells
of the disintegrating mind.
Never leaving completely, and arising in periodic swells
Allowing no joy of any kind.
Tearing into sleep, taking it away so even the strength of rest
can give no temporary quiet to the howling screams.
The inner swirling of panic crushing all within my failing chest
My growing weakness even the plot of shallow dreams.

Who knows where this demonic flame gives birth in those
without the body's mutinous death date?
Vacant loving arms or something buried in the aliquoted geney dose?
Yes, something from inseminated fate.
We still blame the fully sequenced genome, yet cannot find the curse.
Some simple imbalance of the chemistry:
The juices of communication one terminal bathes on other nerves
Supported by improvement for most with well thought pharmacology.

But what about this pain of those for whom we see a cause:
Death of wife or child; irreversible disease.
The downstream recipe may be the same, but this loss
Cannot be softened with the same good tonic ease.
Will Zoloft or Lexapro bring back the child, bring back the wife?
These drugs or any others can't touch my amyotrophic lateral sclerosis.
Will they comfort me enough as I lose my mind and life
through the horrors and hopelessness of progressive paralysis?

Any thoughts of what I used to be are going, fading, gone.
The anguish of what's to come unbearable
Any dreams of what I might have been are now withdrawn;
Accidental images of my aging wife and son so terrible.
I crave a knife, my own hand to pierce my bowels,
to carve up through my useless stomach into my blackened heart.
I long for the gun, the moment before so spiritually foul,
the voiceless terror of what I've become fading part by part.

The instant after, a mystery more welcome than
what remains should I now fail to brave.
Any God who can't forgive this should not be he who hands
out this hopeless and relentless path unto the grave.
And if He can't, if he causes such horrific anguish
and refuses the comfort of its controlled escape,
Then Fuck Him, to begin with, while I vanish.
The cruel joke of a life so shaken from its hoped for fate.

I have read of Joyce's Hell, I could not make it to the end
But I was younger then, and capable
Forever fire, forever separation from the Three of Them
But, this is now the better path than that which is the unimaginable.
Oh, this isn't me, say my loved ones and my friends
"You must fight to the end," even as you cannot move
Oh, I say, take a stroll in my wheelchair, cut off your hands,
Gasp with my failing diaphragm and savor the tastes through a PEG tube.

"Do Not Go Gentle Into That Good Night," say they who care.
Selfish, they perhaps, who cannot tie the hangman's rope.
If loss of wife, suffer for the children left so bare.
If loss of child, hold your spouse for time to cope.
If death impending, suffer the shock and horror so severe
Endure the state you always dreaded most of all
For those who want to cherish him they hold so dear
And the worse of two evils find some how to stall.

(ss 10/28/2009)

Passage

I know what stars are really made of.
I've studied astronomy.
I know of planet gravitational field theory.
Space is bent by massive objects.
Time itself has no rigidity.
But is the cosmos just a bubble chamber?

I eat a steak. I take a shit.
When I look in the toilet,
I see no trace of cow.
I've seen intestinal epithelial cells
in the field of microscopes.
I see where the proteins become me.

I smell the incense. I hear the chimes.
The people from the temples
sell me tarnished food in
the crowded marketplace.
I know the cleansing effect of dysentery.
I was not one with the parasites.

I take myself in my own hand.
I fuse with Satan, as
my eyes roll into my head.
I tell these things unto The Robe.
He chastises me and gives a formula,
while he'd like to have me to himself.

Poetry man has described
so many things that make me feel
I'll be forever joy.
But man appears to ruin all he celebrates:
the woods, the hills, the sea, The Word.
He is the beef within the porcelain.

I try to see the green in brown.
I search for peace within distortion.
I look deeper down than scopes allow.
He separates the wheat from chaff.
When I close my eyes for good,
will I see Nothing, Calculus, or Tat Tvam Asi?

(ss 10/07/2009)

Pessimism

Spinning, whirling, centrifugal blurring all to disappearance
It takes but one lethal diagnosis to obliterate all your past illusion
Tricked into a life-long game of man-made God-ruled ignorance
Played by the mechanistic laws of school to work to black confusion

Breathing, chanting, incense sniffing and Jung reading
Hopeless Bible verses written by diers, read by a droid
Babies die, children die, young poets slash-wristed bleeding
Drink yourself to death dark poet of Providence and fade your infamy to void

A bunch of cells collected and functioning by evolution
Membranes pumping ions, nerves firing one upon another
Just an advanced stage of a river rock, universe pollution
No magic hope as told to starving children by a hopeless mother

The sandwiches you eat will turn to shit or just the dirt
You leave behind when "Heaven" and Orpheus crap on you
Has anyone ever passed and loitered back to give a word
To offer any true enlightened other worldly view

No, my dying beast, like a dog but with the curse of mind
There's no proof of any cosmic juice but molten ash and soil
You were nothing once and that is what you leave behind
A trickle of nostalgia fading as your remnant loved ones toil

(ss 12/7/2009)

Present Awareness

Every golden day of man from first cry on serves to breathe
Flavor into his myriad battles with pondering his decease
Happy childhood, playing games with boys and girls naïve
Will just someday confer resistance to the pre-death feast

The squelching of his freedom by the mechanistic drone of school
Blessed radiance in some of man's great ideas through all of time
Even the magic gift for new found thought, supposed sign of anti-fool
Certainly religion, a lifelong journey driven by man's useless climb
Against suffering, to coat the soul with hopeless balm of Gods and Saints

Early tragic loss, encounter with the dark souls of great poetry
May give a brief glimpse into the mental quest of the terminal
Someday these joyous backgrounds like the presents of the tree
Will just make more gooey hindrance to the boxed inevitable

Maybe as the aging body fails and the hair of the finite turns to gray
More palpable than all past autumns with their browning leaves
You'll be blessed to only then make your not so unexpected way
Into the cleverly put off dreaded journey that your absence weaves
Not into you, as missing as an un-invited guest, but those you loved

Oh, but if premature death comes knocking at your back pages
Maybe when the car bombs of hatred against the modern weapons
Of the arrogant ignorant blast a young man to the near last stages
Or an ailment unimagined descends on youth to start hell's lessons

Then, be gentle, you non-dying, and know that your pretty gifts
Your hoped for normal time with family, a suggested bucket-list
Are sometimes painful reminders of all we were made to cherish
If these are why we're here, then surely thirty to fifty years less
Of all these wonders is enough to realize a loss unbearable

Such loss, of you, and all our past and present treasures
Can only be survived with the killing of a former thinking
There are three paths to the dying mind that releases pleasures
Varied ways to the insanity that can accommodate our sinking

Tragic fear of the finite, one's future void, and the stark horrific
That no poem, scripture, drug or gifts can ever hope to battle;
Blind surrender to fate not avoidable, with an acceptance stoic;
Or hiding in the sand of Spirits, listening to the Christly rabble
Of all your living friends who can't see the blessed madness

Chanting our way to numbness as the cruel biology of Earth
Deteriorates the stupid lipids of our brain, the muscle of our heart
Back to the raw protoplasm of the Fire, Water, Air, and Dirt
Crudest demonstration of the oneness we dreamed we were a part

These divine and glorious concepts may be true; I have belief
But it is the face to face war with terminality that defines all men
The insanity is the liberation; a madness is the narrow path towards relief
Pretty paper wrapped presents and dwindling time with loved ones
Thorazine-like delay of the immaculate journey to morphine-flavored fantasy

Drink ourselves into oblivion; meditate ourselves to catatonic victory
Read the works of our pondering asylum mates who noted they were dying
Why shake us back into the world? The glaze lifts off our eyes, we see
The delightful contents of your gift wrapped world, our rage inside ignoring

To what purpose your pretty presents, joyfulness, and songs of anti-gloom?
Why delay our steady downward progress to the welcome black?
Why remind us what we're losing? Every smile a tulip careless in the sick room
Only the journey into the depths from where there is no coming back
Is the sole thing truly human; the single thing we all will share

(ss 12/22,23/2009)

Formula

You will eat the new, improved milk of the metal house
Your classmates will then replace your lowly Mother
Take your place in the pre-fab maze like a proper mouse
You will advance in common by each being better than the other

Come lad, stand in your shiny trousers against this ruler upright
Press your recipe mind against this paper logos gauge
We have a formula for making perfect monkeys so uptight
It starts with concrete, all right angles, and civil sage

We will build a frame around your insecurity
Out of gossip, the regards and anti-scorn of society
We will attach a tachometer to all of your activity
And measure praise, respect, avarice, lust, and jealousy

You will gain awareness by sacred media guiding
Under whose eye the elected demigods will prance and race
And the gowned Venus and Apollo on red carpet striding
Will be the pixel deities of this new master race

Oh but look, we found this boo-boo in your chest
Hey, don't worry; we have the well made science tools
To save a few months for you at maybe half your best
Lay in the sick room staring like the other empty fools

Let's pass through you these magic beams of radiation
To at least be sure your final heart is placed correctly there
Appears you never saw the inner light for deviation
Took all the wrong turns to make the straight line nowhere

(ss 01/10-12/2010)

Beads

Clear brown child-proof bottle
(Child proof: against the child)
A cabinet shrine
To *Homonis Modernis*
Symbol of science faith

Hope container
Opened twice a day
Capsules (decades of research)
Like unstrung beads
For a rosary

Slow the course
But for your curse,
Just a finger in the dam
Best to celebrate the river
Bathe in the glory of drowning

(ss 4/13/2010)

"Where I come from…"

Where I come from
There were no roses,
But lots of photosynthesis.
There were no parks,
But rows and rows of benches.
Where I grew up
There were no kittens,
But I saw the skulls of cats.
When we made young love
The smell of perfume
Gleamed from the Table of the Elements.
Poems were made of bosons.
The sunset danced on rods and cones
As we sat, hopeful, on endless silica.

(ss 05/03/2010)

Relationships

To Serve

(for Sally's "Walk to Emmaus")

When man is at his lowest, and his mind
and deeds are turned to "lust" and "greed",
A God-man is needed, to teach his kind:
The Love of God, the essence of all seed.

The wisdom of Sophia guided His hand.
Only a virgin, like Nature un-sacked
could give all Her Children of Man
the Son who would lead the way back.

Sin is but only the absence of Him
in one's heart and any daily act.
His message was but a simple gem:
"All are One"; to love, we make a pact.

What suffering, and at such a young age;
Miserable, in pain endured with love.
To restore our Souls, calm Yahweh's rage:
Arisen, to faithful at Emmaus; departing dove.

You now "Walk to Emmaus", with His three
days your focused reminder: never swerve!
It is your blessing now, redeemed in He,
To carry on this wisdom of Love: To Serve.

(ss 10/24/2009)

Ode to Mom

(for Alice on Her Eightieth Birthday)

I

From the tough times of a simple hard working father
The large family of a sometimes overwhelmed mother
A one of many, with so few gifts to call your own
Maybe one new pair of shoes a year from town
To wear to school, with pride despite the other kids
Maybe laughing, having more than your family did
Of some things, but not of all that matters
Love between you, siblings dressed in tatters
A lone candy bar at Christmas, but free to run
In the woods, the fields, amongst the summer sun

II

Leaving school early, the war years, brave your travel
To make your way in the big city on the grand river
Bright you are and always have been, auto-didact
Bashful young dame, blossoming in war's aftermath
Placing your slender figure, great gams, lovely face
In the crispy uniform of the WAC, growing world embrace
Sharing laughs, occasional tears, in youthful fun
With girlfriends, seeing movies, hearing crooner tunes
Catching the eye, no doubt, of many a smitten soldier
Shy, gentle doe, who clicked with he like no other

III

He, the man you married: husband, friend, father
Sharing every moment intensely, first a daughter
A strong force to grow from your baby to a woman
My sister, kind spirit with a non-deterred passion
Then, a little boy, oh how your arms again would fill
My brother, a budding man of principle, drive and will
Then, as if you didn't have enough to do, a third
A little boy, an obsessive, who had to tell you every word
The last to complete your triad of hungry little hearts
You shaped with humility, to serve man in each our parts

IV

Baseball Maiden, giving to all your food and cheer
Den Mother in uniform blue and never tired smile
Always present, for study help or function volunteer
Helped me with my vocabulary and let me stay a while
With you, in bed, day's end and nightstand lights warm
I can still hear the pages of your thick books turn
As I'd nod off, finally, protected from youth's harm
Love given always, something we didn't have to earn
Expanding, challenged, as life as always carries on
And your kids, like others, worldly passions learned

V

Sold houses, woke up sleepy teens caught up in plays
Then watched us leave, to live our own mistakes
Patiently waiting, hoping, praying as we made our ways
Through school, more and more school, money sinks
Took our brief and forever loves in as if your own
And nurtured our babies, your precious grandchildren
Completing a circle of family, with love and wisdom
Settled in Hill Country sun, to shine in rays of Christendom
Your marriage always present, "two silver hearts"
Glowing in a lifetime commitment, a love unquestioned

VI

But where to now dear mother, aged and wise
Your child is struck with a fate you cannot make
Go away in a few days, with juice and blankets
Doctor's trip, note for school, nasty orange syrup
But, do not fear for me, and do not tear for me
You have already given me all that I will need
To pass on to the next stage that all may see
If they know the love of He in whom you raised
Your children, in whose Grace you lived your life
As Teacher, Protector, Comforter, Mother, Wife

VII

I won't live as long as you, lucky me if half plus ten
But the love and guidance that you have given
Has allowed me to live a life richer, fuller than
Any other, no matter when or where I may have risen
You taught me to be kind, to love and to accept all men
To be strong and brave, traits I carried with me always
Even the years I was too strong by science driven
Now we reach a time where on this earth our days
May not be long as dreamed by youthful Son and Mother
But we are prepared for an Everlasting Blissful Other

VIII

Hymns loft out of all the Church's roofs and windows
They rise from the hearts and souls of all God's folks
Children, young wives and mothers, old men and widows
Their devotion carries like the warm breeze through Live Oaks
Gently your thoughts stir of this, a joy filled passing phase
You watch the burnt orange, red, and lavender of sunset
The peaceful end His Hand delivers at close of each our days
Tomorrow we rise, give thanks to all we've known and met
We carry on; we make this and the next journey together
All in peace, all in love: as taught by our Dear Mother

(ss 11/27/2009)

I Reach Over

(for Heidi)

I reach over; empty sheets, an empty comforter.
I grab the smell; a temporary solace, a twinge.
In the shaded light, I see your half-naked silhouette.
In awe of you, and you on me, I see your back arch slightly,
    your arms bend,
As you cover your breasts and our new-found mutualness,
    for the outer world.

I doze, I dream; I remember with eyes closed.
I feel warm painted lips, lips for the outer world.
In clothes like pajamas we don't use, you leave to mimic your day.
In distraction from you, and you with me, I bend my back deliberately,
    in my tasks to hide from you.
As I cover my heart, and the implications,
    for my inner world.

I bend, you don't break. You break, I mend. We fuse.
I love, you love more. You give, I give enough.
In time, that mythical delineator we all underestimate;
In years of you, and you with me, we come back to us, we glow
    in the world of our.
As boys go up and down, as grapes go in and in,
    we live a secret world.

I stumble, I fall. You brace, you stand tall. We pass.
I question, I anguish. You question, you stay silent and strong.
In another clock, in another heaven, we can't realize;
In a world we breathers may call perfect, with our backs
    against avīdyā,
As I go on forever, you go on forever, and we know
    or want no other world.

I wipe my tears. You feed me, very well.
I pray, I search: A permanent solace, a wing.
In darkness, an incense-jaded hope, a green prayer.
In the knowledge of you, in the essence of us, I cry out
    in all directions.
As I reach over, I add bliss to bliss, love to love,
    and we move on.

(ss 9/29/2009)

Spring: From Lubbock to Colorado

Champagne masks a face familiar
Bubbles turn a smile into a buffer
Towards a life cut sharply out from present
And a future fading from commencement

Flat, forever flat, and gray
While the normals resonate with crickets
I'm eternally enmeshed in concrete
And new brick shoes condemn the feat

Migrate to majestic mountains
Make an ethereal connection to the clouds
The viewers and shapers proceed to play
And send some shooting stars my way

Snow as white and foreign as birth
Glazes the grandest ancient calling peaks
Almost reaching the pure placental sky
A narrow gap for primal childish cry

(ss 5/15,17/2010)

Old Love

I dreamed green fields that stretched forever
Like the ones I ran in growing up
Dancing under summer sun, the infinite warm rays
Laughing on my head full of hair and innocence

Electric kisses tasting like a secret sip of wine
Filling my exploding chest with tragic thunder
The first steps upon a hidden planet, changing
Forever the destination of a sacred journey

Soon, the rains come, blindness washes way
Daily beaches are sabotaged by boulders on the shore
Fires fade, cold ashes pile like granite tear drops
Monuments to yesterday in museums of hard regret

Old birds perched on an elegant branch held up
In a tree drawn by the toothless smiles of children
Plots turn like unseen winds on a barren hill
Of a gothic tale and slowly fray the edges smooth

Psychic warriors search for just a glimmer of a smile
Remnants of a magic code once held by only two
One last fragile stroll on the glowing blades of sand
Holding hands, again, welcoming the pierce of sunset

(ss 5/08/2010)

Moving Within
and Upward

Words and Blankets

Words come easy when you're dying;
You can throw them out for all eternity,
For everyone to ponder or ignore.
But, they help you feel like you have learned something,
That you are leaving gifts behind.
You may be right or you may be tragic,
But it helps you live each passing day,
Despite the knowing: that your time has come,
As horrific as a prisoner on death row.
Is it better to know your exact date,
Or just your pathetic fading state?

I don't like to be completely covered;
I get warm, I need some air to pass over me,
To bring me movement, to know that I'm alive,
To feed me like a moving shark who only rarely comes
Completely still, not by choice but maybe fate,
An inner knowledge that nature moves the ocean currents
Around and through him, to feed his ancient primal needs
Of nurture, blessedly without knowing that when all
The movement stops, only the blanket of still waters,
Of wool, of aerating knitted afghans,
Of cotton, yarn, and breeze remains.

(ss 11/15/2009)

Ouch and Love

I

Ouch!
What gives?
I can't stand
to think what is
happening to me.
I was supposed to be
some sort of magical child,
with brains and heart to give to all,
with special science and care to balm
the grief we have held that grows forever.

II

You suck!
Force divine
To steal from me
And all I walk with
My heart, my work, my spine;
To now prematurely claim
The glory you yourself installed,
And strike me down like a flower starved;
Piece of feces strewn into manure.

III

Hey, I hurt!
And, I am scared.
This is not the pact
I, at least, signed up for.
What are you trying to teach?
Can I count on a something next
That you will share to make it worth all
I have given in this working call?
If you rob three decades, can you share more?

IV

God, what I've seen!
Worse, what I've thought of.
Jesus, can you spare me?
Krishna, love, give me a break?
I struggle; I've got more to take.
What's the deal, there's more to foil;
Let me hang around with mortal coil.

V

I mourn, my soul aches!
I search for some reason.
Why then have my little cells
Died before their rightful season?
Have I been so bad, have I not done
Things at least as good as those ancient ones?

VI

I become paralyzed!
My body slowly decays.
My mind seems to grow and to swell.
And so we come to some encounter
I can't win, you're too big, so I engage.

VII

I search far and I read long!
No answers come from clever books.
In the dark of mystic cerebrum,
I look for divine paste that holds all men.

VIII

There, a flicker, a giant void!
The floor, the walls, the ceiling give way
You enter, small, subtle, kundalini.

IX

Light that can't be explained in quanta!
Every night I've read, I've studied, I've prayed:

X

Now, it explodes, inside, spreading outward!

XI

We are only, and always, cosmic juice!
But that is heaven, and all I need.
Psychic facts, real as physic proofs.
Wife, child, family, all men:
Part of ever wholeness,
Even if not seen.
We move on, preach
The Word, You
Peace, dove,
Love!

(ss 11/19/2009)

Perspective

If you step, you may just fall; if you run, some day you'll stumble
Better to lie within vast solid walls, where no light can all encumber
Best to not encounter, to not compete, and stay so humble
Shield your heart; it is only to pump the blood to keep your slumber

If you read, if you listen, you may well fall prey to cherish
Beware not to smell the flowers on the neck of any love
Brace yourself against the guise of life with one who just will perish
Strengthen guard to myth of nature and stupid hope from up above

If you follow just these simple rules you can pass this wretched life
But few can live within the dark fortress and not soon venture outward
Beautiful faces, exquisite food, tides, meadows and poetic sunrise
Soon you like all the fools believe you matter and begin your claw upward

Then you learn and feel so smart; rise as man, collect some things
House, car, written word, sung song, and clinging clothes
Everything you do, all that you have…look: this is of Kings
Race against time; define yourself against the decay carved within His laws
Every walk in the forest, each holiday shared will all be lost

The lion will kill the lamb and you his flock in horrid vacant flashes
Happy faces of your friends will show your fate in smiling ignorance
Each thing you sought and all you held cannot go toward your ashes
Regarding all as one, now and always, is no more help than just avoidance
Either can calling all illusion erase the first pain in your mortal circumstance

Instead, fellow traveler, see the smiles as the pillars of your journey
Shared love between friends is not a prize, these emotions are an atlas
Grant to all the unknown walkers of the earth your new soul's hard forged key
Owned things are fading things; pleasures were granted to remind each of us
Divine are facts learned and passed, felt words shared, to spread a warming bliss

(ss 12/13/2009)

All the Temporal Colors

I – Time: Fundamental Time

In the moment of the beginning of time
With the ruby-blue hue of the magic of rain
Overhead in the mystery thunder of divine
I ran with my sharpened wood over the plain

My raw feet of urgency impressed their transience
Kicked up a stone of polished raw core of earth
Where two red-purple slimy earth worms coalesced
In a passing dance of moist hermaphroditic future birth

II – Time: Radioactive Time

The glistening furry tan brown of marble deer
My hopeful chase into redeeming red-brown meat
The smiling white teeth of the hungry children near
Parallel the temple columns of gray cerebral inner seat

Murky brown waters of my sweated harvest offers
Floating down under factory charcoal tinted gray
Unto the grizzled marketplace, plastic rainbow proffers
Hard work hypnotized into hard times, empty souls dismay

III – Time: Luminescent Time

Bouncing golden curls, a fair maiden's naïve ballet
Hiding under a net of un-protective electronic interaction
Crimson, mauve, maroon, brown, black, the blackest of your pallet
Stamped out virgin mystery for nothing gained in green transaction

Broken legs and open mind within the highest orange of energy
My brightest penetrance; blistered eyes against vertebrate encounter
Golden flakes from our tainted past to cast shadows so severely
Through our shattered hearts, lifting piece by sharper piece to something rounder

IV – Time: Please, Time

(ss 12/27/2009)

Outsiders Heading To The Grass

A seven-legged spider climbed up my kundalini
And stopped for a breath of fresh urban smog perfume
Before it could reach the exit hole on my head
Labeled "Shoot Me Here"
It choked on a designer neck tie from some silicone
Infected blow jobber.

Spherical coordinates of probabilistic knowledge elixirs
Yell fire in the already un-crowded temple theater
Now I can't rob the donation plates for my glacier driven
Pimped-up Astro Train to Cirrus Minor
Guess I'll have to pray for the death of prom queens
While I lick up the city five-star mucus fragments
From the pavement garnished with the smack needles
Of the discarded rejects who were beaten to a juiced
Neuronal pulp cocktail of apathy for societal consumption
Before their anti-biological bitch inseminators allowed them
To make it to page two of the Concrete Life instruction manual.

Fermented nectar from movie land ego presses
Crawls down the squamous mucosa that we invented
To keep the artificial ingredients out of my jack-in-the-box.
Opium circles flare up the limbic nostrils and
Curl along the hidden passes of clouded cingulate guides
Mescaline curtsies to the Neo-cortex pseudo demi-god
Discharging the lovely re-channelings her oozing lubricates
Dung incense of primal buffalo hordes care less of social judges
Water towards.
Water, processed water, filters through the nephrons of my
Temporary dwelling.
Flows down the leg of one with the detachment of the secret knowledge.

Walt ejaculated sticky insight on occipital lesion leaves
Demoniac selfish spleens drive factory droids
Careful with that gas Adolph, don't push extermination
To the point of truly global innard searching.
Leather souls of the fancy political stompers
Stamp, stamp, stamp the butts of their decorated park
Sealed envelopes licked with forked tongues
Of the stairwell guarded adipose cheek protected
Anal extruders of atmosphere clogging pollution.
Shaven heads mystify another unwarranted safe landing
Metal flowers bark the impatience of their enslaved masters
The padded malls coax smiles from imbecilic oral buttholes

Exiled poets with frozen testicles hold
The official party of the last laugh
Vedantic cobwebs trickle down the Broca sewer
Like golden dysenteric particles hidden in a cave
Confessional bards hide in a special purgatory
For the enlightened sobbers of overdose
Their realization too unbearable for prime-time
Where tits in tight tee-shirts hypnotize
The ass-kissing brain-dead masses.

What's a seer to do? Trapped at the lowest level
of the planetary system of the cherished garage infusion
Silver forks put the blackest coal into the blacker hearts
You see the truth, you gasp and hush your useless lips
Save it for the ex graduate students so they can dream
after selling shoes all day
How does zero point zero five live between the lines
of blinded keepers of the firearms attached to monkey brains
Slash the wrists of this silly corn-stalk tamale sheath
Offer the corpuscles of your un-saleable insight
To the Ganges of the bathtub next to the porcelain
Of the obvious and limited

Lay down in the steamrollered lotus position
Of the gradually disminded
Open your eyes, then gouge them out
With the sharpest end of your secret ray-gun
Then finally see the stars; feel the small proper
Six and eight-legged philosophers douse you
With the Holy Water of tragic future human protoplasm
Enjoy the essence of the dribbling beauty
Your teachers and their flag-waving masters
Beat from out your sacred heart

Smell the magic of the dark; shatter the synapses
As you always knew they were falsely plugged
Into the box of illusion voltage
Rearrange them according to the wart-hog wrist schematic
And the long lost plan of the cinnamon bun giraffe neck
Listen to the chlorophyll drone of ecstasy
Please, Keep On the Grass.

(ss 12/30/2009)

Dance

It was the winter of my Prozac solstice.
My material body had ridden to Miami
In the back seat of an old colleague's 1977 Malibu.
Matilda came waltzing over from across the misty room,
And noted that I had spilled some Dostoevsky on my lap.

She smiled a perfect smile, which scattered
All the gray holiday dust from underneath
The dark seats of my side of the room.
In radiant eminence from her punch lip-sheltered
Crisp white enamel Venus temple columns
Erupted the words of my heavy mud-stained boots:
"Can't you write a happy poem?"

I slowly raised my neck-bound head
And looked up into the crack of pale yellow
In which her earthly manifestation was enmeshed.
I peeled six layers off my previously assembled space suit
And wiped my crotch clean of its transparent protective soul paste
I took her lovely age-appropriate hands into my restructured remnants
And uttered my useless elegy:

"I was happy with the energy of my youth,
Playing with my friends real and made up games until the dark.
I was happy for my mother's warm smile,
The shelter of a loving and supportive family.
I was happy for the smell of silly dogs,
For unquestioned companionship of love untainted by motive.
I was happy for backseats of heart-racing awkward moments,
The butterfly dance of new and uncertain love.
I was happy for the way the sun that soaked the beach all day
Nestled on the water's edge at the reach of my eye's horizon."

The lovely dame who'd absorbed so much of my decline
Like a sponge with the scaffolding of a museum
Then raised yet another mirror to my gray and black reflector shield,
"Would you like to dance?"
Partly, near completely, closing the shade
On her entry through the constellations,
I reminded her that my legs didn't work.
Squeezing my finite fingers just more tightly,
Beatrice laughed a gentle tug of last minute solace, saying:
"Silly poet, don't you know yet
That we dance with our souls and not our legs"

(ss 12/31/2009 – 01/01/2010)

Divine Slap in the Face

My left foot no longer moves, so what's the good news?
There is none, Scott, you clinging fool; why should there be?
It started at the hip, moved to the toe, the leg's as good as dead
You spent all your life climbing to the top, and in your last step
Cruel fate punished you for all your past deeds or just the hell of it
You had the biggest dreams of all time and you were on your way
Now you are just a tripping fool for others to feel sorry for
And guess what, sucker, we're only just beginning on the paralysis trail

Oh Dark Lord, Doctor, I have been your kind, I have cared since I began
Why do you, of all people, shake the blackness in front of me?
I am young, I have so many things, and I can collect more while yet
I can give more, I can accomplish so much it makes the saints look impotent
Why poison me? I'm the poster child for humanity: ego and accomplishment
Hey Mother Fucker, whoever you are, my right toe is starting to get weak
And now my right foot, my previous proud right leg, the faint twinge in my arms
They're following down the slightly delayed parallel hideous functional amputation

Fuck. Damn. Shit. Pseudo God of hopeful lives with no real hope. You suck!
I am as transient as a daisy on the dress of a virgin on prom night, pussy moist
I am a flicker in the undecipherable swarm of cosmic humid mental moisture
Who was in charge to let me create this fantasy of a long rewarding life extraordinaire?
I will die a pathetic death of incompetence in all the things I took for granted in your world.
You cock-sucker illusionist with nothing real to offer. I'm as brief as the cream in your coffee.
I have a wife, as beautiful as the glint of sunshine on the early morning beach
I have a son, as precious to interact with as the dawn of the first steps of all mankind

Hey Scott, I know you're listening, because I gave you your ears, I gave you a stereo
I gave you a mind that makes the flint look like it cannot a spark give forth
You clueless little douche bag, your blindness I did not inflict keeps you from the truth
I gave you more than all the others. You had so much; no one could hold it all too long
You have received more love from all sources than any little human could endure
You have thought more than any brain is physiologically entitled to without bursting
And still you fight instead of love. I like your angry spirit, but it is time to channel it
To what you should have always realized: you think, you love, you marvel, you're blessed

Your hands still move, you little shit; they can caress the cheeks of your beloveds
Your mind works like the well greased prophesy of Isaiah or the late night words of Blake
Quit feeling sorry for yourself. You are not transient. That stupid little body I gave you is.
You are immortal. You are not canned goods. You are soul juice that comes back to me
But don't piss me off any more. You have a couple more years in your silly skinny form
To spread the word of my Love, to earn what I will give you for time you cannot dream of
Each moment amongst my creations is an eternity of appreciation for my eternal love
Why do you think that a wheel chair made by caring men is any different than your finite legs?

(ss 01/13/2010)

She

She walks on the air, not because she is aloof
But rather, she floats within its layers
Dances in a love for which she has no proof
Her hello radiates the colors of true fairness

She is removed from all the false world passions
Flowers touch her hands like lotus blossoms on a pond
Engaged in warmth, sparks grow in all her interactions
Her smile takes strangers to the sky and far beyond

She lives in the forest on mountains of strangeness
The trees swell their barks by just her to and froes
If she doesn't command the rivers' ocean progress
Her grace makes the water happy as it flows

(ss 01/14/2010)

The Assassination of Physics
by the Unknown Aqua Man

One autumn night my restless spirits took me to a local bar
After several drinks and never ending numbing small talk
I stepped out into the alley for a leak and hoped-for fresher air
I came upon two men in vigorous debate, the scope of which gave balk

It must have been the faint illumination of the clouded moon
But whereas the older suited gentleman was pale with glasses dense
The lovely younger man appeared almost blue and spoke in tune
Harmonious his gorgeous voice, so I crept to secret audience

Glasses: "We discovered particle physics and quantum theory"
Blue: "You came to realize that all is one, a cosmic energy"
Glasses: "But we can now mathematically model and manipulate"
Blue: "Schrodinger can't get you much past hydrogen; you've made bombs of hate"

Blue: "We gave you the names of all the Heavens and their Gods"
Glasses: "Fairy tales made up out of ignorance on the hopeless trods"
Blue: "Perhaps these beliefs were far more useful than your theories"
Glasses: "We've disproven all this myth, answered mankind's greatest queries"

Glasses: "We know fields give mass, time is relative, laws vanish in black holes"
Blue: "None of which you've 'proven' by methods precious so outside your souls"
Glasses: "But we model some and you have nothing like the particle accelerator"
Blue: "Your science covers but a grain of sand on the beach of Life's Creator"

Blue: "The sacred content of your God's holy words can do much more"
Glasses: "How is that possible, no mathematics can even now explore?"
Blue: "The descriptions of the Heavens and God's play on earth impart
        more than your empty quarks in putting love into your heart"

Glasses: "How can I kill what is inside me that blocks me in this path?"
Blue: "A long time ago, a demon appeared as a giant serpent with great wrath
        Into his mouth went my friends; I entered, expanded, and he did burst
        But from my touch, he fused with me. Now, take off your glasses first"

Then with one of his four arms Blue hit Glasses with a conch shell
His head exploded, but rather than gray matter mixed with splattered blood
Golden radiant beams and particles without properties to hypothesize and tell
Entered the chest of this Aqua Man, whose smile a universe could flood

A most interesting event indeed, and so I wandered back inside
Maybe coffee was in order, but I asked for lotus blossom nectar
As the bartender took my hands in his, I felt a bliss I could not hide
As I sipped the quenching knowledge, I felt my Blue Lord near and far

(ss 01/19/2010; 02/07/2010)

Hare Krishna!

The Waters of Purgatory

I died on a Tuesday
It was probably p.m., as I was always a night person
On Thursday, I had a weird dream
I was being escorted through a foggy landscape
By a beautiful maiden that reminded me
Of maybe Liv Tyler or perhaps Audrey Hepburn
I think her name appeared to rhyme with Minerva
But it seems pretty sketchy now, as
After all, I was still trying to come to grips
With that whole dying thing

We walked gravitation free over a peaceful savannah
Until we came to a small pond of pale gray smooth water
She called it The Wisdom Pool
When I asked her what it was for
(After all, part of smoothly dying is assuming
That everything has a purpose), She reassuringly responded
That each time a human being does something
Wise and helpful, he or she automatically makes
A deposit into this heavenly repository
From which anyone past or present can make
Non-depleting withdrawal to help them or others
In the otherwise challenging struggles we daily face

That being said, as we quickly passed around it
On our leisurely stroll, I was surprised at how
Small it was compared to an adjacent steaming ocean
Sensing my next question (as I had been a scientist before),
She informed me that this was The Selfishness Pool
Each time a man or woman did something for
Only their own benefit an equal aliquot as per act
Was sadly added to this vast sea that seemed to go on
Forever

As we walked along the shore, our bare feet in the sand,
I asked if this was Heaven
Of course not, she said smiling, and to use language
I might appreciate; she said it was basically a triage stop
And then I noticed a scurrying amount of commotion up ahead
She seemed embarrassed and as if apologetic, explained
Each disturbing scene and activity that we passed beside

There was a famous physicist with the universe's
Largest particle accelerator in his anus making
New elementary particles out of his intestines
There was a celebrated molecular biologist
Whose testicular tubules were stretched out
The precise length of the human genome sequence
Printed out at a convenient 10-size font
I recognized a Hollywood movie star
Who was being made to explode as many times
As the dollar amount he received for all his roles
I tried to nonchalantly wipe a piece of his warm
Lung tissue off my cheek as we continued on

Apparently, with his presumed demolition expertise
And all the majestic brains of these past successful men
They were trying to make a channel between
The ocean and the pond, to no avail

(ss 1//29/2010; 3/06/2010)

Moving Within and Upward II

Collapsing

Shrinking…fading
Imploding – in every direction
Inexorably dedicated to atrophy
A fragmenting shell braced towards Hell

The myth of the past
Exposed in a brilliantly exploded
Time and space changing revelation
Of the Neuromuscular Guillotine

Adjust…adapt
Rearrange – in all misdirection
Is there a Phoenix to be found
Made of more than cells and atoms?

(ss 2/4/2010)

Conversion Order

One morning, as rigidly registered by sun-nourished man
The former physical form formerly known as I
Woke up (that is, I transitioned from my dream state)
And I could not see a single thing, not a hint of form
With the ophthalmic globe units and occipital cortex
I was issued upon my trans-placental eruption to this Earth

Horrified, expectedly, as in this state I could not function
Within the world I had so skillfully crafted
In collusion with my self-empowering culture mates
Before I could pour my synthetic breakfast
Out of a Styrofoam container into a plastic bowl
Dr. O.T. Sucsamad showed up into my door

Although I don't recall having called him
Or even having ever truly known him
I suppose my secretary could have put him in my speed dial
"I can fix your vision", said this strangely smelling fellow
"But it will cost you…you as you are now…a huge price."

Without hesitation, I agreed full heartedly
As I eagerly reminded him that in all my life
All I've ever wanted to do is see things, see everything
Completely, the way they really are
With all my scientific guided curiosity

Acknowledging our pact without bringing up financials
He touched my closed eyes with his warm fingers
And I sensed a slight tingling followed by
A not unacceptable amount of burning
Pleased with the process thus far,
I then received a blow to the back
That so disrupted my expectations
I felt that I had been twisted inside out
"What was that?" I gasped in the direction
Of this most non-traditional physician
"The price you agreed to", he replied, as if reminding me

"But don't worry", he added in a voice as strong as steel
 But somehow as warm and comforting as real milk
"I'll be with you every…step…er…every part of your journey."
I sensed he was departing, but I couldn't tell as he'd
Neither made any noise upon his prior entering
And so I loudly uttered, "How long is this to take?"

In the same voice, but as if it were coming
From inside or even up above me
"About a week. Everything, it seems, takes about a week"
Then after a brief pause, "Of course, it could seem
A lot faster or maybe even so much longer
After all…what is the word you people use
Ah, yes…it's all *relative.*"

The first day, I saw only red
I saw the blood of all the beasts
I saw the anger on men's faces
Yet, I couldn't even find a cardinal

That night, I could not move my toes.

The next day I saw only orange
I saw a raging forest fire
I saw hot lava destroying villages
So, I prayed for one lush sunset

That night, I could not move my legs

The next day I saw only yellow
I saw jaundice in the eyes of a sickened race
I saw the cowardice of blabber mouths
But, I could not find the sun in a field of chickens

That night, I could not move my arms

The next day I saw only green
I saw piles of money in the center
Of skeletal selfish rabid grasps
I saw envy as the mask of much politeness
I ran as fast as monochromatic vision can,
Still, I could not find a single meadow

That night, I could not move my fingers

The next day I saw only blue
I saw ischemia of dying toes and brains
I saw the sadness of broken-hearted lovers
Yet more sadly, I could not find a single patch
Of clear sky in the Maya monsoon

That night, I could not move my neck

The next day, I saw only purple
I saw the velvet robes of artificial royalty,
Disconnected from the cries of hungry peasants
I saw the livor mortis of every man past killed in war
In the haze and rain I looked for the Life-
Flavoring flowers of the passion fruit

That night, I could not move my lips

The next day, I saw full colors of the current rainbow
I saw the white man kill the red man's buffalo
I saw orange flames emit from intercontinental missiles of hate
I saw the yellow of tear gas quieting the mouths of freedom
I saw the green of toxic waste strangling the breath of trees
I saw the blue of a flag spreading superficiality over all the globe
I saw the purple of exploding hearts of hopeless poets

That night, I could not swallow

As my quivering body faltered
Away this meaningless state
All my senses changed and wrapped
Together round my budding cortex
As each fiber died, a cosmically shared neuron
Awakened in anti-entropic instant counter spin
Concrete emptiness echoed like a
Computer generated scream in a pantheistic temple
The latest topic of celebrity gossip shows
Sounded like the disconnected babble
Of previously encountered psychotic delusion
In the sacred wards for the not quite maladjusted

Now, I cannot breathe

I see universes budding in clouds of
Gas from the belly of the cosmic vacuum
I feel intergalactic waves resonating
A thousand octaves below Bach's Air Suite
I hear the wisdom of our ancestors emanating
From the holograms in the pillars of expanding space

I see my former body lying in a pile upon the floor
In an infinite time your own transient forms
Mourn my brief farewell
A sacred cow passes its soul into ancient vortices
Spinning, fusing with the future of a little boy
In the guiding microwaves emanating from God's kitchen
At the zero time and filling the space between
Two new planets in a galaxy you'll never "see"
An organizing resonance from a billion universes gone
A memory of a pleasant exchange between two aliens
Fuses in a divinely guided interference weave
With the smile I received in the grocery line last Thursday
And with the emotion of a kiss between two primal
Lovers in the first universe of the walking fishes
A zillion ages after protons made love in the hydrogen dance

I am there and you are there
You and I are not You and I
We are God
Instantaneously connected illusory fragments
Coming and going, forward and backward
In a flux of indescribable all permeating ecstasy
Bound only by lawless Unity

(ss 1/28/2010)

Remote

I hobble down the street
like a peg-legged searching pirate
uncomfortable on dry land
where my modified appendage
may sink like forever lost treasure
in the sand blinding everything around

I sit at a café table
surrounded by the stares
of animated robitrons
I feel like an off-set nun
in a bikini contest
where the most beautiful cannot be shown

I gaze at the grass and trees
fused into a blur
of gold-tinted never green
My gouged out vacant eyes
see only the piercing white
of the cosmic flame I can't perceive

I twitch like a rapist
in the electric chair
on which the invisible
used to sit so casually
I am connected
by only a slender hidden thread

(ss 02/11/2010)

Questioning the Nightly Sickbed Visitor

Where do you come from late at night
When all the well-wishers are gone and
The quiet swells among the grim reminder?
Do you blow in upon the breeze of the
Slightly open window next to my special chair?
Do you seep up from the floor boards,
A soil presence emanating from the core of Earth?
Do you glow from out the giant plasma screen,
A molecular ectoplasm from the quantum world?
Do you blossom from the nectar of the open bottle
Of this otherwise delicious age-softened Pinot Noir?
Do you arise from the pages of my books,
Called forth from the right combination of words,
Growing like a genie out of a heart-felt poem?
Do you come from the words of a Dylan song
Playing in my ears the scaffolds keeping me upright?
Or do you come from all of these, a consequence
Of some ancient alchemical blend synergizing
From all these different hopeless bandages?
Why are you known exclusively to me?
Why do the others here only stare
At me when I try to explain you?
Where do you go to during the time of day?
Do you hide to build your strength
For your tragic and most thankless task?
Or do you haunt another's solitude
Maybe in an Oriental zone of time?
Why must you be a secret?
Do we have things to be ashamed of?
Or is your palpable transparency
A gift to only those making the grand transition?
What is your purpose when you
Emerge from nowhere into the sparsely
Decorated living room of my searching mind?
And why do you sometimes take me
Up and sometimes take me down?
And how come, sometimes…often,
I can't tell the difference?
Why must you take all of my prior ideas
And jumble them, as if the soup of my former
Existence wasn't worth the bowl I've put it in?
Why does the path the crow flies
Seem so circular to me?
I never know where we are going
When I close my eyes and you take my hand.

(ss 4/26/2010)

Ice

I am just chipped away
from the myth
of the structure
I was promised

In the material world
of physics
and evolution
Robbed of stature

Among family and friends
I am thin
within the blocks
Of humanity

I am only shadow
now precise
soon to melt
I am a swan

(ss 02/12/2010)

Essence

I am not the wall; I am the window

I am the forgotten poet
imprisoned for a vision of oneness
based on true concern, but arrested
and beaten by the closed-mindedness
of the power hungry hidden avarice

I am not the map; I am the breeze

I am the fall of a leaf
into a mountain stream, its flow
through the hills into the river
of the valleys and bustling towns
until it reaches the mighty ocean roar

I am not the fence; I am the gate

I am the first steps of an
awkward colt, the flow of milk
from mare to future radiant stallion
patted not just rode, and running free
in the grass from which I am the smell

I am not the mouth; I am the smile

I am play of the little boy
and the pain and tears of his
wounded knee, the bandage kiss of
sacred mother; storehouse of memories
of all the fathers' fathers' fathers

I am not the old man's legs; I am the lap

(ss 02/18/2010)

Warmed Over

I am the crazy cousin locked inside the closet
The one only talked about in passing hush
Mythical mutant pondered in your bravest moments
Beast of the other world touched in the safety
Of a campfire enclosed by firmly set up tents

I am the wind that makes you pull the covers up
The scratch of tortured branches on your window panes
Black covered book buried still beneath your bed
Scarcely opened in a dare, and never really read
Of darkest tales that bend the spine upon a pole

How long can you hide from me, you have to wonder
You've seen my magic in the graveyard and your dreams
You will never rest if 'gainst me thou must brace so hard
If you must squeeze your eyes so tight it breaks the light
I will rise like a fog that steals your every breath

Greet me, make me known, and introduce me
Go upon the hill and in the silence of the night
Say hello and do not turn away as if I'm ugly
Live in fragile peace with me and all that I may bring
And I will grant your soul the rest of sunny days

(ss 3/28,30/2010)

Telescopes

We go to bed with the rings of Saturn in our eyes
The perfect blend of love and sweet technology
We saw such stars as we never could have seen
Magnification, like breath,
One of man's great solved mysteries

We are powder, coalesced on transient frequencies
With the wind, with the moon, with a core
Deeper than our most truly expressed whims
By our thoughts then, we alight
But it is in our quiet that we radiate

I glaze in your presence, a jumble of Light
Formed like a perfect sandcastle
Out of patience. I wave an unintelligible farewell
The tides will lift me on their shoulders
Like a long lost cousin carrying my coffin

To a secret party made of fuzzy animals and sunshine
Like the scent of descending Lotus blossoms
Almost foretold by scrolls and telescopes
I was here…I was here until I was no more
And then with you, with the stars and planets,

Something more.

(ss 5/22,25/2010)

Cruel Teacher

A pilgrim to the nether lands of open-mindedness,
How could I have lived underneath this veil so long?
What kind of worm would have blindly allowed its
rigid placement?
Crawling along the earth, a slimy piece of darkness
Imprisoned in a cage I did so much to weld
the iron of.
A pilgrim to the nether lands of open-mindedness.

My love lies dim like the ulcer in a beast
Punishing the tortured viscera of its selfish hunger
As if living out the well-earned Sisyphean
curse of gods,
Who would one day raise their vibrant voices
In the penetrating stars of a celestial
"told you so".
My love lies dim like the ulcer in a beast.

Death, like the brightest candle shines
Upon the deepest, buried rotten roots,
The gnarled and twisted hidden feeders of
our tragic hearts.
Late the blossoms come to forgotten Eden where
Limbs wither under the pressure of awakened
golden sunlight.
Death, like the brightest candle shines.

Mortality, cruelest teacher and jealous keeper
Of the secret key of a kindest radiance
That releases the carefully constructed barriers
of the mind,
And removes restraints of open arms I offer now.
Tardy and perhaps too late the molten ashes
cleanse the soul.
Mortality, cruelest teacher and jealous keeper.

(ss 5/26/2010)

On a Clear Day One Can See Forever

Crystal clear are the details of the distant mountains
Seen through the gifted vision of the crispest sky
Transparent despite its deep divine soup nature
As clear as the sparkling sea a thousand miles away
But as connected as the virgin snow on the highest peaks
Joined by a common primal and purposeful past
Before we became their displaced progeny

The scattered junipers sprinkled on the rolling hills
Join the rugged range and their bathing clouds to me
Like connecting quantum dots of irreducible botany
Neither here nor there, just where they need to be
For now and where I see them in this passing moment
Berries to needles, branches to roots, Gnostic soil
To ancient rocks layered by the greatest artisan of time

A hundred billion galaxies with a hundred billion stars
In perhaps an infinite number of unknown universes
And yet, our little crumb is thoroughly complete
Landscape set upon a sage-painted seasoned stage
From the burning sun down to the darkest burning core
The majestic mountains to my bare and calloused feet
Perfect before me...Perfect briefly with me...Perfect evermore

(ss 6/04/2010)

Impressions of a Shortened Physical Life

by Simon Hayward, Ph.D. and M. Scott Lucia, M.D.

For the second time in my life I am engaged in the somewhat unusual task, for a professional scientist, of writing a supporting section for a book of poetry. In both cases this has been for a friend; however, more sadly on this occasion, for a friend facing the reality of his own mortality. I first met Scott Shappell a decade ago while I was interviewing for a position at Vanderbilt, and we worked closely together for several years until his move into the private sector. His interest in academic problems was undiminished by this change in employment and with his typical high energy levels he has continued to contribute to various projects. As a result we have been able to continue to interact and publish together.

My interactions with Scott have been, first and foremost, in his role as a clinical pathologist with a particular interest in diseases of the genitourinary tract. Specifically I work in the area of the biology of prostate cancer and benign prostatic disease. This was also Scott's professional focus. This background in medicine and science inevitably informs his outlook on life and occasionally crops up in his writing. Scott's tremendous energy and enthusiasm for the various projects which we undertook was a critical driver in broadening my horizons. He got me involved in a number of studies which continued in my laboratory after his departure. He was instrumental in making me take an interest in fatty acid metabolism in prostate cancer, and the manner in which this controls the differentiation and proliferation of tissues. This links existing treatments for diabetes with potential activity in controlling early prostate cancer growth, and has become a major project for my research group. This has also resulted in a project linking obesity, diabetes and benign prostatic hyperplasia, common co-morbidities which may be amenable to integrated treatment approaches.

Scott always wanted to fulfill more than one full time role. In particular his position as a professional clinical pathologist with all of the associated diagnostic responsibilities was not truly compatible with his desire to also run a research laboratory – another full time job. He managed to walk this tightrope for a number of years, essentially by extending his working day. One of the curious features of interacting with Scott was always his personal take on when the day began and ended. For him a given day often ended after many people had already started the next. Receiving e-mail (often several pages of e-mail) from him in the not-so-early morning hours was routine. This method of working, of course, could not go on forever and some years ago Scott moved out of academic medicine for the relative sanity of starting a new company to deliver molecular and clinical diagnostic services. There is clearly a certain irony that starting a successful company can be considered a move towards a less insane working week, but this really reflects the amazing energy that Scott always put into his academic career.

Outside of his professional life Scott has a personal existence. His interests include one of the best stocked personal wine cellars that I know of, along with a broad knowledge and passionate interest in the subject. He and his wife Heidi (also a pathologist) also showed enough dedication to their two large dogs that, on moving to Dallas, they invested in an independently air conditioned dog house allowing the dogs freedom to the outdoors during the day while also providing them with a cool space to which they can retreat. Scott's son Travis (a student training to become an architect) along with Heidi, are clearly the two people most directly impacted by his health issues. However a serious disease suffered by a friend and colleague affects a much larger group of people who, even at a distance, sympathize and grieve along with the patient and their immediate family.

Simon Hayward, Ph.D.

As a physician scientist, I am comfortable with the writing of scientific papers, reviews and commentaries. Yet, the words that I write now come with great difficulty. It's not the content that gives me pause, for I am honored to be able to tell my story, but the process involved in its telling. We physicians are taught early not to wear our hearts on our sleeves and this writing is personal not scientific.

The world of academic medicine is competitive and, at times, oppressive. As such, establishing close friendships within the practice of academic pathology can be difficult. Finding those in "the biz" whom you can love and admire as friends and seek to emulate professionally is rare. I have been extremely fortunate in that I have had a few such relationships amongst fellow pathologists. The first was my mentor of 12 years, the late Gary J. Miller, M.D. Ph.D. Gary was held in particularly high regard in the scientific community for his pioneering work in the biology of prostate cancer. His manner towards his peers and students of pathology and health science was remarkably collegial and inspiring. As a practicing pathologist who specializes in disorders of the genitourinary tract, I have modeled my career after Gary. Unfortunately, he passed away at the age of 50 while I had still much to learn.

The second person who has greatly inspired me is the author of this work, Scott B. Shappell. I met Scott while we both were part of a research consortium that was assembled to study benign prostatic hyperplasia, a disease of the prostate that affects a large number of aging men in the U.S. I immediately felt a kinship with Scott that I had not experienced with other scientists or physicians. His intellect and brilliance as a scientist was immediately evident, but that is not what intrigued me. It was his openness and genuine interest in those around him – something I hadn't experienced before in a collection of scientific "experts". I made it a priority to get to know him. What I found was a man of strong principles whose path had remarkable parallels to my own beyond sharing the name of "Scott".

We both graduated from college with degrees in science in 1984, Scott from the University of Dallas and I from the University of Denver, and entered into medical school the same year. Scott completed his M.D., Ph.D training in 1991 and chose his path as a physician scientist early. I was bent on a career as a practicing pathologist but got bitten by the research bug during my residency. We both became academic pathologists that specialized in disorders of the male genitourinary tract (prostate, bladder, testis) and kidney. Notably, Scott had expertise in the evaluation of kidney biopsies for medical conditions such as inflammations and functional disturbances. This is an area of pathology that a very limited number of pathologists practice, but of which I am one. The combination of expertise in genitourinary pathology and medical kidney is rare indeed, and yet we shared this commonality.

My fondness for Scott has intensified as our scientific collaborations continue. Scott is a forward thinker who never allows himself to be contained by the "box." His ideas have always intrigued me, and he often unselfishly serves them up for the rest of us to act upon. Even as I write this, we have ongoing scientific studies in the area of prostate cancer that we anticipate publishing.

Yet, it is his want to think and live outside the box that eventually led to Scott leaving academia and go on to establish his own commercial laboratory, Avero Diagnostics. Scott has always had tremendous insight into what makes an outstanding medical laboratory. The degree to which a laboratory can expand and accommodate the needs of its clients is often impeded in the academic setting. A number of factors are responsible for this such as limitations on cash flow, operational organization, and a multiplicity of missions including research, education, and clinical service, all requiring administrative support. Since we academic physicians usually have our time and energy split between these missions, it limits our ability to truly focus on any one aspect. Also, as salaries in academia are fixed, the incentive to market and increase patient load is lacking. Private enterprise has the benefit of focusing on the single purpose of providing the best patient care services possible to the greatest number of patients. For Scott, this meant more freedom to excel in the area of patient care where he was most passionate. Yet, unlike most private labs (and largely due to his almost insatiable appetite for work), Scott maintained a strong research arm in support of research directed at patient care, helping to establish new technologies and laboratory testing procedures. It is through these ventures that I have had the good fortune to cultivate my relationship with Scott, and my life is richer for it.

Though their talents as physicians truly amazed me, what ultimately drew me to Gary and Scott was that they chose to be people first and then professionals. They achieved what many of us still struggle for – balance, the ability to live life to its fullest. Gary was an outdoorsman, nature photographer, gourmet chef, and family man. Likewise, Scott is an avid reader, music lover, and wine connoisseur. As humanitarians, they both cultivated relationships that went beyond science and medicine. Their examples have reinforced in me that to be human and mortal is not a weakness but what makes us dynamic, holding the power to improve our world.

Nature doesn't always play fair. Bad things happen to good people. We have each been given a certain amount of time to invest here on earth. The people who seem to contribute most to the world are often the ones who stay the shortest time. But their investment pays off, not only for the richness that they experience in their lives, but in the gifts they bring that enriches their community and those around them. This book is but a small example of the grace of an extraordinary man. It is appropriate that it is shared with those suffering with the same fear and turmoil that Scott has come to understand. Gary and Scott gave me a wealth of lessons and experiences that have made me a better person. I will forever be grateful for our time together.

With love and respect,
M. Scott Lucia, M.D.

Spiritual Correspondences

This section consists of a series of correspondences contained in emails between the poet and his older sister Sally. The time period covered is approximately the second half of 2009 (roughly corresponding to the first several months of the composition of the poetry included in this volume), beginning approximately 5 months after Scott's ALS diagnosis. Many of the correspondences originate with a spiritual quote from Sri Ramakrishna or Swami Vivekananda, offered by the poet. As the author began his spiritual journey following the development of ALS, he was especially attracted to certain Hindu teachings. Brief introductory backgrounds for Ramakrishna and Vivekananda are provided here.

Sri Ramakrishna was a humble God-man who lived in India in the 19th century and who spent much of his life in a God-intoxicated state. His teachings contributed to a new spirit of recognizing the equality of all religions, a message carried forth by his disciples. Ramakrishna was born with the given name of Gadadhar in Kāmārpukur in 1836. After a spiritual childhood in a rural setting, he followed his eldest brother to Calcutta at age 16. He served briefly as the priest of the Temple of Kāli (the Divine Mother) built by a wealthy widow at Dakshineswar (near Calcutta) on the Ganges River. However, his abilities were interfered with by his essentially constant God-intoxicated state, including visions of the Mother Kāli. His spiritual bliss led many to think he was insane. In the course of his life, Ramakrishna was instructed (including by passing spiritual teachers) in Tantra, Vaishnava disciplines, and Vedantism. He obtained realization of God and the state of samadhi through these approaches, as well as through the practice of Christianity and Islam. He would spend his life at Dakshineswar in the worship of God. He passed on his spiritual awareness and divine wisdom to visitors from all over and a steadily growing number of devotees. He is most commonly associated with the approach of Bhakti-Yoga, the ecstatic love and desire for God. He died at the age of 49, apparently from throat cancer. The words of Ramakrishna included in our correspondences can be found in The Gospel of Sri Ramakrishna, including Abridged Edition, Translated into English and with an Introduction by Swami Nikhilananda; Ramakrishna-Vivekananda Center, New York; original copyright 1942; Seventh Printing 2005.

Swami Vivekananda was born in Calcutta as Narendranath Datta on January 12, 1863. A very intelligent young man with fine singing skills, he had started college in Calcutta, the main site for the entry into India of European ideas. In part to counter Christian missionary influences, Hindu reforming organizations such as the Brāhmo Samāj had been formed. However, young Narendra found no satisfaction for his spiritual quests in these movements, and through his ongoing Western readings was becoming essentially agnostic. Frustrated by the inability of any acquaintances to answer the question if they'd ever "seen God", he was steered towards Ramakrishna. Ramakrishna told Narendra that he sees God as plainly as he sees him, and literally knocked him unconscious by his holy touch. Narendra spent his young years as Ramakrishna's cherished devotee, a natural charismatic leader in whom Ramakrishna clearly saw a divine purpose. Upon Ramakrishna's death in August 1886, Narendra and a group of other young devotees founded the Order of Ramakrishna, now the largest order of monks in India. From 1890 to 1893, Narendra served under a variety of names as a wandering (begging) monk, which allowed him to see first-hand the great spirituality, but also the severe poverty, of his fellow countrymen. He felt that his country could benefit from Western technology and that the West could benefit from India's spirituality. The young monk took the name of Swami Vivekananda shortly before his first trip to the West in September 1893. Two years of lecturing in the United States and Europe allowed Vivekananda to carry his master's message of the universality of all religions. He founded the Vedanta Society of New York in December, 1895. He acquired many Western followers, some of whom became established devotes. He finally returned to his mother India in early 1897, where his devotion included more focus on works as well as spreading the message. The newly formed order established the Ramakrishna <u>Math</u> at Belur (where it still exists as the major center for the order today) and the Ramakrishna Mission, which set out to establish schools and hospitals. A second trip to the West included California and involved the establishment of more Vedanta centers, including in San Francisco. He returned to India quite ill, at which point he longed primarily for spiritual quietude, including at the Advaita <u>Ashram</u> in the Himalayas. He spent his last years in deep meditation until he died at the the age of 39 at the Belur Math on July 4th, 1902. Western readers of Vivekananda have included George Harrison, novelist Christopher Isherwood, and the recently deceased writer J.D. Salinger. The words of Vivekananda included in our correspondences can be found in Teachings of Swami Vivekananda, Published by Swami Mumukshananda, President, Advaita Ashrama, Kolkata India; copyright 2004.

As a bit of personal background, the poet, older sister Sally, and older brother Steven were raised as Army Brats in a Protestant family. Sally is currently an active member of a Presbyterian Church. Steven subsequently converted to Catholicism. However, after leaving home for college and then medical school, Scott no longer participated in organized religious worship. Following undergraduate education, he did regard mathematics and physics in a broader concept related to order in the universe. However, in the increasingly pragmatic world of medicine and biomedical research, he became farther and farther removed from the beliefs that he had been exposed to in his early life. Scott increasingly embraced the reductionist science belief that everything (all the way up to memory, emotions, and free will) would be eventually explainable by science. Confidence in experimental science may be inexorably linked to conviction in one's own abilities necessary to succeed...in one small component of one cog in a very large number of wheels, not particularly compatible with pondering the "larger" questions, per se.

When diagnosed with ALS and being forced to address his finite nature decades prior to expected, Scott realized the crucial need to address his spiritual life. Some of the beliefs he has acquired may be resurrections and expansions of some earlier deeply held notions; some may be new. It is possible that this journey may not have commenced without these pressing and all-or-nothing circumstances.

Since these correspondences were undertaken in the setting of facing challenges initiated by ALS (potentially relevant to a terminal illness in general), we hoped that they may provide at least some warmth and love to others facing a similar challenge, either personally or by the equally demanding position of being a loved one supporting physically and emotionally a person with ALS.

We do not profess to be experts on any of the topics discussed and the opinions are strictly those of the writers. These correspondences were the spontaneous thoughts and reflections of the authors, highly engaged in dealing with the difficulties and implications of a life shortened and complicated by ALS. As such, they have only been minimally edited in order to retain a certain frankness and emotion that is potentially more human and more useful than a highly polished scholastic work. Occasional clarifications added during editing are included within brackets [ ].

A Glossary for some Hindu and Vedantic words and some other potentially unfamiliar terms is included at the end of the book, with included entries underlined when first used in this section or in the later Book Reading list. We thought that since the correspondences are centered on universal messages from enlightened minds, seeing all religions as equal paths to God, that they would have broad appeal. As these are often commented upon by Sally in the context of her Christianity, they should have particular meaning for Christians, who of course, are more common in our country. Yet, the presented thoughts may even highlight the similarity of the messages of love and God-searching shared by the two great religions of Hinduism and Christianity and broaden the avenues of great messages for mankind. Recognizing the universal need for the love of God and/or at least the love of fellow man in this temporary physical Earth journey can only help those dealing with the added burden of the challenges ushering in the premature death of the typically decent folks fire-bombed with ALS.

As our Indian mystic friends teach us, the sole purpose for life on Earth is the realization of our relationship to God. That journey can take many paths and that realization can come in many forms, from ecstatic love of God and mystical liberation to enhanced celebration of the time with our loved ones. For our fellow ALS patients, you will have already begun or soon will begin to see the world differently...in a way that makes you special indeed. As hard as it is to believe, this road block to normal life may reveal a blessing in the detour on a very bumpy road that leads only to Light. Everyone is going to die. Most will eventually suffer. If any aspect of your condition can help you see the true meaning of life, you are, in the end (which is just the beginning?), better off.

Our consciousness is part of a truly universal Divine consciousness, a state of knowledge and bliss that we are here to help celebrate in manifested form and to learn how to return to it in purity.

If our thoughts can be of any comfort or inspiration to any others, then we feel further blessed. God love you all, brave souls.

ss 2010

—ɯ—

Sally (Tuesday, June 2, 2009 12:17 AM)

Here is the list I prepared while at your house but couldn't forward to your email there and couldn't print out at your house. Heidi, if you end up printing this out for Scott, please tell him to place this list inside his Bible so he can keep it handy.

Thanks,
Sally

HELPFUL SCRIPTURE

Psalm 20; Psalm 23; Psalm 27: 1-6; Psalm 32: 7 (pertains to fear); Psalm 34: 11-22 (18-19 pertain to suffering & death, depression); Psalm 38: 21-22 (pertains to prayer); Psalm 39: 12-13; Psalm 40: 1-10 (pertains to depression); Psalm 41: 3 (pertains to sickness); Psalm 46; Psalm 84: 10; Psalm 91 (especially 1-6); Psalm 107 (pertains to resentment, gratitude); Psalm 112: 7-8 (pertains to fear); Psalm 121; Psalm 136; Psalm 146; Proverbs 3: 3-6 ("Trust in the Lord...," pertains to worry); Proverbs 4: 1-27 (pertains to worry, wisdom); Proverbs 27:1; Isaiah 12: 1-3 (pertains to fears); Isaiah 26: 3-4 (pertains to worry, illness); Isaiah 41:10, 13; Micah 6: 8; Matthew 7: 7-8; John 11: 25-26 (pertains to eternal life); John 14: 1-3 (pertains to depression); John 15:7; Romans 8: 18 (pertains to eternal life); Romans 10: 17 (pertains to faith); Philippians 4: 12-13 (pertains to trust); James 4: 13-17 (pertains to prayer); James 5: 16 (pertains to prayer); 1 Peter 1: 3 (pertains to faith); 1 Peter 5: 7 (pertains to worry, fear); 1 John 1:19 (pertains to prayer)

—ɯ—

Scott (Wednesday, August 26, 2009 11:01 PM)

"One is aware of pleasure and pain, birth and death, disease and grief, as long as one is identified with the body. All these belong to the body alone, and not to the Soul."
-Sri Ramakrishna

OM! Peace. Peace. Peace

Sally (Thursday, August 27, 2009 10:34 PM)

This one I especially like. Back home from Santa Fe since about 6:00pm - had a great time. Will talk to you more tomorrow – have to get back to the real world tomorrow unfortunately.

[Returning from Santa Fe refers to the tail end of our second post-diagnosis RV trip. Scott, Heidi, Sally, Kel, and Travis took a 40 foot A-class RV from Dallas to Arches National Park, UT, Zion National Park, UT, Grand Canyon National Park, AZ, and then back through Albuquerque, NM and Santa Fe, NM. Sally stayed on in Santa Fe for two days to attend outdoor opera with a friend. The trip was very pleasant. Arches and other destinations allowed for some reflection on Native American spirituality and the beauty of Zion and Grand Canyon are humbling reminders of our place in Nature. These reflections were a continuation of a process started with a first RV trip that included Great Sand Dunes National Park and Mesa Verde National Park in Colorado].

—⚹—

Sally (Thursday, August 27, 2009 10:37 PM)

Mary [cousin of Sally and Scott] will be on her ALS fundraising and awareness walk Saturday, through her church in Alabama. They had their dinner last night and included a prayer for you. She raised her pledge money and the walk is through the local ALS chapter there. She is dedicating her walk to you, wanted to let you know you are on the prayer chain there.

Scott (Thursday, August 27, 2009 11:44 PM)

Is there a way we can support her walk? I'll take the prayers!...but there are those with ALS and other motor neuron/muscular diseases in a less favorable financial situation, so if we can give to her to spread it around, let us know.

Likewise, telethon for MDA (which pays for our clinics/equipment, etc) is coming up... tell her thanks

love, ss

Sally (Friday, August 28, 2009 9:56 PM)

I already donated/pledged for her walk sufficient to bring her to her total - I have a link if you want it (I have created an ALS file folder in my email folders and can forward it to you, which may have more info about donating for future walks).

Sally (Sunday, August 30, 2009 11:23 PM)

Thought you'd like to know this

Forwarded from Mary Mast (Sunday, August 30, 2009 7:51 PM)

Sally, I just wanted to thank you all again for your support of me in the ALS walk. Jack [Mary's husband] and the girls also joined our church team. We hosted a spaghetti dinner on Wednesday night at church, and had a great day at a nearby stadium for our walk (Jack, the girls and I did the entire 3 miles). All together our team raised just over $1100 for ALS support and research! Thanks again for helping us to make that happen.

mary

—ɱ—

Sally (Thursday, August 27, 2009 10:39 PM)

I won the ALS/4Major League Baseball [MLB] auction and a base plate from the Tampa Bay/Texas Rangers baseball game is on its way to me, the money going to ALS! This is what I was talking about when we started the RV trip.

[The base purchased by Sally was used in a game over the July 4th weekend during which MLB was commemorating the 70th anniversary of Lou Gehrig's retirement and his famous speech, which included reference to his ALS illness. The base was signed by Hank Blalock and Carlos Pena. Sally became aware of this auction via an e-mail from the Alabama ALS Chapter. She had been added to the email list as a result of her donating to our cousin Mary's ALS walk, as noted above].

Scott (Thursday, August 27, 2009 11:47 PM)

That's great! I still think you and Kel should either put it on a rock near the house or on top of the <u>butte</u>, or something, as a meditation/monument sort of thing. Do you know if it's a base (square and couple inches think) or home plate (5 sides, flatter)? You could also make a bar stool or telescope stool out of it... I look forward to hearing scope stories/finds soon.

[Scott had given Sally a telescope as the last opened of 50 presents he gave her over a period of weeks, including during an RV trip, for her big 50th birthday on July 18, 2009-at which point she and our family pronounced her the official village crone, in recognition of her age and acquired wisdom]

Sally (Friday, August 28, 2009 9:59 PM)

It's a base, not home plate. I do like the idea of using it as part of a seat for a meditation seat/spot near the butte, maybe surrounded by a juniper tree. I used the telescope last night and got a great view of the moon - but didn't find Mars. Kel said this weekend we will get the computer set up for the scope and do more viewing.

—⟋⟍—

Scott (Tuesday, September 1, 2009 1:56 AM)

"In like manner one who constantly thinks of God can know His real nature; he alone knows that God reveals Himself to seekers in various forms and aspects. God has attributes; then again he has none."
-Sri Ramakrishna

This is what I love about Ramakrishna and his message. Although he believed the <u>Vedas</u> and had achieved samadhi in the rigorous <u>non-dualist</u> approach, he had no problem seeing God as the Absolute (without form, as in the classic <u>Vedantic</u> Philosophy), yet also God as having attributes and filling everything and everyone around him. This manifested God WITH attributes Ramakrishna increasingly appreciated, particularly the presence of God in men, as his illness progressed. As God manifested in infinite ways reflects the essence of Bhakti, then to me, it seems that if you truly love God, the rest is just "details". No one can understand <u>Brahman</u> (as indicated in Vedantic philosophy, but not inherently different than the concept of The One God in other religions). We can only approach It (God) by accepting It and trying to appreciate It by It's manifestations: man, animals, nitrogen-deprived bonsais [alluding to Scott's apparently suffering newly acquired plants], Grand Canyons, etc; but I will continue to strive to see God directly.

peace, ss

Sally (Tuesday, September 1, 2009 11:16 PM)

I really like this one - and your comments. I think there are passages in the Bible that even address this concept; that is, God without form...as God beyond our comprehension, yet God also in all creation and in every one we meet. This is one reason why we must learn to treat all individuals as our brothers/sisters or at least as well as we would treat ourselves since there goes God as well.

Scott (Tuesday, September 1, 2009 11:40 PM)

Ramakrishna was a believer in Christ and his message, as was his disciple Swami Vivekananda. I agree with your comment about treating all others with love, and I hope that I have been kind to others as I have progressed through life. Although it seems that a strong sense of spirituality (as we're alluding to) could impart such love for one's fellow man, I have also come across some interesting psychological explanations for why individual men and women may sometimes (or even often) act otherwise. From reading about some of Jung's concepts of the Shadow, some of the things that we repress or we need to reach towards in the unconscious for further development, we may project onto others (as characteristics) and then dislike them accordingly.

In addition to personal examples, there are potential larger examples in society (which would thus be much more difficult to encounter and "fix"). For example, the "English Gentleman" concept of the 19th and early 20th century and the need for "savages" for the completeness of that societal construct may have contributed to colonialism and the way the English colonials behaved and treated the natives. (This supposedly could have accounted as well for a noted higher than expected S & M behind closed doors of English society and homosexuality arising out of the English educational systems at that time). Whether one believes it or not, another example that involves an even higher number of cross societal humans is the Christian oversimplification of Evil. Personifying Christ as perfect and embodying all good was easier than recognizing the complexities of his true Self and his message. Thus, if we are likewise pure good, then there must be evil elsewhere...not in ourselves of course, as certainly not in our God (a huge misrecognition according to Jung)...causing or potentially causing us to do evil. Hence the need for Satan and the (projection-based) recognition of evil in cultures/races not like "us".

I find Jung's concepts of Evil amazingly insightful...but that's not the point here....it was more regarding the message of "Love Thy Neighbor as Thyself", which got oversimplified as a "Golden Rule". Yet, to follow it always is largely impossible when regarded only as a "practical" moral code (like some law against J-walking or such), rather than the potentially (questionably more likely) intended meaning by Jesus, which you allude to as in seeing us in all others, and all others in ourselves. This sort of real enlightenment or wisdom makes for true tolerance and unselfishness. The accidental or purposeful misunderstanding of some of Christ's messages is one of the greatest tragedies of Western Civilization. [See also *The Gospel of Thomas* in Book Reading List]

There are those who see the spirit and love in Christ; there are others who saw and still see an oversimplified excuse to feel superior and tread on others and to regard some wonderfully spiritual races and individuals as inferior. I suspect it makes Jesus sad. All one can do is act according to their heart with the goodness they know is right....and maybe someday, somewhere, the good spirits will finally make an impact on the self-centered power hungry ego driven manipulators...and we will know peace and love to some fraction in this life that we know will come with attainment of Existence-Knowledge-Bliss Absolute in our Souls, here and now, but in a maybe purer form in some other plane.

peace, ss

Daily Ramakrishna - in keeping with recent theme...

"Does God exist only when I think of Him with my eyes closed? Doesn't He exist when I look around with my eyes open? Now when I look around with my eyes open, I see that God dwells in all beings."
-Sri Ramakrishna

Sally (Wednesday, September 2, 2009 2:41 PM)

I like that new quote - makes me think of the act of praying with your eyes closed, as many think one must do (questionably, a visible sign of piety). I do usually bow my head in Church when it is time to pray, but often it is because our pastor has just given us some morsel to think about and I do this better with my head down in concentration. I think originally the idea was that one can focus better without the distractions one would see with eyes open, but if I am wanting to "see" God when I am praying - why can't my eyes be open? By the way, our Sunday school class year starts 9/13 and I am taking a Christian Meditation class with Suzanne - our Associate Pastor who I took the Spiritual Practices class with last season and who I was in Santa Fe with last week. Will be interesting to see what is presented.

Love and peace and grace – Sally

Scott (Thursday, September 3, 2009 1:35 AM)

"As is a man's meditation, so is the depth of his love. As is the depth of his love, so is his gain; And faith is the root of all. If in the Nectar Lake of Mother Kāli's feet My mind remains immersed, Of little use are worship, oblations, or sacrifice."
  -Sri Ramakrishna

Sally (Thursday, September 3, 2009 10:11 AM)

Wow - this one is great. Thanks for sharing. I have been keeping these, so I can pull them up when I want to read a little helpful quote.

—ɷ—

Scott (Friday, September 4, 2009 12:59 AM)

"There are two characteristics of <u>prema</u>, ecstatic love of God. First, it makes a man forget the world. So intense is his love of God that he becomes unconscious of outer things. Second, he has no feeling of "my-ness" toward the body, which is so dear to all. He wholly gets rid of the feeling that the body is the soul."
  -Sri Ramakrishna

(I'm working on this one....)

Sally (Friday, September 4, 2009 2:49 PM)

It's so hard because everything around us is geared toward focusing on the body and perfecting the body and beautifying and worshipping the body - yet the body is so imperfect and feeble and fragile, and only the soul is infallible and can become perfect. But the man-made society looks outward and we need to spend time trying to get each other to look inward where beauty lies and where unity and wholeness and connection to each other lies. I am sure it is a struggle but you seem to be working very nobly on this matter - it takes most people a lifetime even when not faced with your particular struggle.

I love you and your efforts – Sally

—ᶜᵚ—

Scott (Monday, September 7, 2009 10:22 PM)

"Some are born with the characteristics of the yogi; but they too should be careful. 'Woman' and 'Gold' alone are the obstacles which make men deviate from the path of yoga and drag them into worldliness. Perhaps they have some desire for enjoyment. After fulfilling their desire they again direct their minds to God and recover their former state of mind, fit for the practice of yoga."
-Sri Ramakrishna

(quotes like this sort of hit home to folks like myself I think)

Peace, ss

Sally (Tuesday, September 8, 2009 11:03 AM)

But I don't think you were selfishly totally consumed by lust & greed - you didn't pursue these with the goal of hurting others and turning your back on all else. You were never one of those who "got to the top by stepping on the backs of others" or tossing people aside - even now, when most people would be concerned with themselves, you are looking out for your family/loved ones and your co-workers & employees. And you are working on the issues of your soul and your connection w/God.

[Sri Ramakrishna in referring to 'woman and gold' was using symbolic terms for broader references to lust and greed. Ramakrishna was by no means creating an anti-woman cult or sexist attitude in his devotees. In fact, the opposite is more accurate. In the background of the social norms of the 19th century, the Master had a very unique, respectful, and essentially devotional attitude toward women, and encouraged his female devotees to act in the same manner as the more common male devotees, warning them against the dangers of 'man', meaning lust, in the same fashion. He had a life-long spiritual relationship with his younger wife Sarada Devi. She was known as the Holy Mother and became an important part of the religious environment and teaching at Dakshineswar. Ramakrishna, in general, regarded women as manifestations of the Divine Mother (Kāli), which impacted the way he interacted with women. He received Tantric training from a visiting brāhmin woman. As he himself embodied many of the tender traits of a woman, his female devotees tended to regard him as one of their own and interacted with him as a child, or friend, or teacher. However, as his teachings were recorded by male devotees, in the readings available to us, we consequently get warnings against the dangers of lust as 'woman' only.]

Scott (Thursday, September 10, 2009 12:53 AM)

M [the householder devotee who was the scribe for *The Gospel of Ramakrishna*, referring to the Master's thoughts and comments]: **"And you are seeing God inside yourself"**
Master: "Both inside and outside. The indivisible <u>Satchidananda</u> **- I see it both inside and outside. It has merely assumed this sheath** [body] **for a support and exists both inside and outside. I clearly perceive this."**
-From *The Gospel of Sri Ramakrishna*

OM
peace, ss

Sally (Friday, September 11, 2009 12:17 AM)

Since we are all creations of God and are all part of God, He is inside and outside - and if we could all remember that we are all part of God and God is inside all of us, we would remember to treat ourselves better (take better care of ourselves, treat ourselves with better respect) and treat others better - show respect for others as they are all part of God as well as we are - no less and no more than we, not lesser beings than we in spite of our color, race, nationality, job, education, etc. Peace and have a pleasant evening

—ɷ—

Scott (Friday, September 11, 2009 2:32 AM)

"I am not asking you to give up all the 'I'. You should give up only the unripe 'I'. Renounce this 'unripe I' and keep the 'ripe I', which will make you feel that you are God's servant, His devotee, and that God is the Doer and you are his instrument."
-Sri Ramakrishna

This is, of course, part of the Bhakti approach, which I think Ramakrishna is most associated with despite his attainment of samadhi through both <u>Jnana-Yoga</u> and Bhakti-Yoga...amongst other "paths". I'm not sure which is easier or which is harder; both are difficult, but worth pursuing...as that's all we can do... as The <u>Upanishads</u> teach us "He who thinks he knows It not, knows It. He who thinks he knows It, knows it not."

Sally (Friday, September 11, 2009 2:32 PM)

Part of my <u>Stephen Ministry</u> training taught us that we are not the "cure" givers - that is God's role. We as Stephen Ministers are God's servants walking alongside the other person during their grief or need. We are acting as God's instrument in the caregiver role to bring them close enough to God so He can offer them what they need. Our material emphasized this often, because it is so human to think that "we" can fix everything and there is a tendency when dealing with someone who has a problem or need or hurt to offer them solutions rather than just to be with them on their journey and let them find the appropriate solution. Serving our role is very humbling because you are reminded that "you" don't fix their problem and "you" don't have the answers, but it is also very freeing to know you aren't expected to have them - you are only expected to be a friend, to care for that person and be a source of God's love and caring to them.

I love that you are sharing this with me. I keep my *In Search of God* book of poems in my purse and read it while I am at lunch at work or waiting for Kel somewhere, etc. I've noted several favorites already. Take care

[*In Search of God* is a collection of poems by Swami Vivekananda, given by Scott to Sally as one of her fifty 50th birthday presents.]

Scott (Friday, September 11, 2009 11:38 PM)

I have enjoyed some of the Vivekananda poems as well. I've been reading a couple chapters of The Bible, then one Vivekananda poem pre-sleep after I go upstairs. I am almost done with Job...I may read Jung's *Answer to Job* sometime.

Regarding the quotes from Sri Ramakrishna, you will love it when you read *The Gospel of Ramakrishna*. There is no greater expression of love, and you will find the beautiful messages in keeping with how you already feel...and it is somewhat exotic given the setting and descriptions of life in 19th century India. After that, it makes sense to read Vivekananda's works.

It sounds like the Stephen Ministry is a real vehicle for meaningful help; not earthly-centered promises of unreachable false expectations. Spiritual health is more important than physical health.

Along the lines of God as the real doer, let's see if I can find another related quote from Ramakrishna (I wrote down some favorites in "My Little Green Soul Book", while I was reading The Gospel. I also got a four volume hard bound first edition of The Upanishads as translated by Swami Nikhilananda (who founded the Ramakrishna-Vivekananda Center in NY and translated *The Gospel of Ramakrishna*). Let me know if interested in the latter....as Upanishads may make a good gift as our various holidays approach...and nice to support the center, etc.

I read the Isa-, Katha-, and Kena- Upanishads in a paperback version Heidi had [See Book List]--the most beautiful sacred texts I've ever read....

From Ramakrishna:

"'I' and 'mine'-these constitute ignorance. 'My house', 'my wealth', 'my learning', 'my possessions'-the attitude that prompts one to say such things comes of ignorance. On the contrary, the attitude born of Knowledge is: 'O God, Thou art the Master, and all these things belong to Thee. House, family, children, attendants, friends, are Thine."
-Sri Ramakrishna

peace, ss

Sally (Saturday, September 12, 2009 2:32 AM)

I would enjoy reading the Upanishads; and I do like the additional quote. I'm trying to get rid of the possessive words - so much of what we have we don't need anyway and we didn't get by any true gift of "our" making. My secretary at work is new here, having recently moved from Salt Lake. (She was excited that we spent so much time in Utah on our second RV trip and that we enjoyed it). Since being in CO, she has been in a car wreck, and as she and her four kids were in the process of moving from an apartment in a bad area of Colorado Springs to Pueblo where her fiancé lives, she had her purse stolen (with all her ID). The storage people in Utah are demanding more money from her to release and move her stored belongings - so she and her 4 kids are living in a new place with very little stuff. Our office collected funds for her to help, and I offered her dishes, mattresses, etc because we have stuff in our buffet and in our basement that we haven't used in 5 years! "My stuff" needs to be shared with those in need because we don't need a lot of the stuff we have. I could go off for an hour on this topic, but it's late and my back hurts and you don't need to hear my soap box on pet peeves.

Love - Sally

—ɯ—

Sally (Sunday, September 13, 2009)

Hey, where is my Daily Ramakrishna?

Scott (Sunday, September 13, 2009 12:52 AM):

"And you should always discriminate between the Real and the unreal: God alone is real, the Eternal Substance; all else is unreal, that is impermanent."
-Sri Ramakrishna

Sally (Sunday, September 13, 2009 4:54 PM)

Thank you - and we should always remember what is important - the Real, God, that is what is important.

—ɷ—

Scott (Tuesday, September 15, 2009 1:36 AM)

Tonight I mourn for the death of Patrick Swayze. In addition to his obvious place in our popular culture and the memories we have of his movies, I always had the impression he was a good man. A horse enthusiast, a fellow Texan, and a loving husband married to the same woman since ~ 1975 that he met when they were both so young. God takes so many good souls (from this form) so early.

"Is it possible to understand God's action and His motive? He creates, He preserves, and He destroys. Can we ever understand why He destroys"
-Sri Ramakrishna

(not saying this literally in some sort of application to Swayze, as we believe the soul goes on forever, just felt like a quote that reflects our inability to grasp why things aren't the way we "want" them, etc)

Sally (Tuesday, September 15, 2009 9:35 PM)

That is indeed the hardest part of our Creator to understand - He created us and loves us, so why put us in a form that has such limitation and fallibility? I always liked Patrick Swayze even in the less than great movies - 1st movie Kel & I went to together was Ghost w/Patrick Swayze. He never did seem like the typical Hollywood guy and always liked that he was from Texas (Houston I think), incredible dancer, and like you said - a horse guy.

One day perhaps we will understand - when we in this form have ended and have moved on to another form.

—ɷ—

Scott (Wednesday, September 16, 2009 2:26 AM)

"Don't find fault with anyone, not even an insect. As you pray to God for devotion, so also pray that you may not find fault with anyone."
-Sri Ramakrishna

Sally (Wednesday, September 16, 2009 9:31 PM)

I am trying to work on this one. I catch myself criticizing far too often; expecting too much of people, but who am I to say what should be expected of people, who am I to set a standard and to judge? I am certainly not without flaws and too many times have not put out my best effort either. I have been told that sometimes the criticism toward or fault we find in others is really a defense mechanism because we are lacking in something ourselves or have failed in something and are deflecting blame. This concept from Ramakrishna is similar to the Biblical advice about not pointing out the speck in your neighbor's eye when you yourself have a log in your eye.

Scott (Thursday, September 17, 2009 12:39 AM):

Yes, that is the Christian doctrine it reminds me of ("the speck in your neighbor's eye...") and I agree with your other comments. As I mentioned, I recently read about the Jungian concept of the Shadow Archetype. Not only do we encounter things that may be missing in ourselves in our dreams, and initially fear/resent them, etc, but these same Shadow characteristics can be projected onto others. In which case, we then dislike those individuals because of their display or possession of the aspects of ourselves we've buried or haven't developed and hence dislike. This can impact cultures at the collective level as well. The problem is this can then lead to regarding all those NOT like yourselves as "Evil"...leading to things like Christian Crusades, etc. Religion, like oversimplified political feelings, can readily lead to fanaticism, and organized religion assumed as national identities can lead to dangerous actions.

Probably all religions are guilty at some point. Despite criticisms of the caste system (which most people don't understand the origins or intentions of, including out of cultural and social necessity during centuries of foreign occupation, not to mention establishment by foreign invaders to begin with....), Hinduism supposedly was/is liberal regarding multiple religious paths. But, that didn't stop Hindus fighting Muslims, in addition to vice-versa. (Incidentally, Ramakrishna and other Hindu reformers were against the caste system.) The unity of religions and the validity of all paths [to God] was one of many of Ramakrishna's teachings. It was picked up as a major message of Vivekananda's, and eloquently expressed to the West. Unfortunately, even if mass media had been available in 1897-1900 to spread the word further, I'm not sure it could have prevented WWI and other things he essentially predicted. I wish more focus internationally was placed on this type of message [such as that of Ramakrishna-Vivekananda]. We don't need new sects, we need tolerance and for everyone to realize we're all seeking the same thing, just with different names and trivial details.

Knowledge and understanding obtained by a few enlightened/naturally loving souls regarding how people should get along and sharing that knowledge freely is not the same as having it emerge in the world of ego-laden, self-preserving politicians though. Maybe we can all hang out with love in some other plane....

So, on that theme:

"I see people who talk about religion constantly quarreling with one another.....They haven't the intelligence to understand that He who is called Krishna is also Shiva and the Primal Shakti, and that it is He, again, who is called Jesus and Allāh. 'There is only one Rāma and He has a thousand names.' Truth is one; ...All people are seeking the same Truth; ...Everyone is going toward God. They will all realize Him if they have sincerity and longing of heart."
-Sri Ramakrishna

peace, ss

Sally (Thursday, September 17, 2009 11:04 AM)

I really, really like this quote - thanks. Also enjoyed the info on Ramakrishna and Vivekananda (and Jung) - will soon be done with other books I'm reading and can start those books you gave me. Take care, happy reading.

[Katy notes that a particularly good book related to the topic of religion and associated fanaticism and violence is *Terror in the Mind of God: The Global Rise of Religious Violence, 3rd Edition (Comparative Studies in Religion and Society, Vol. 13)*, by Mark Juergensmeyer.]

—〰—

Scott (Saturday, September 19, 2009 12:10 AM)

"When one develops love of God, one needs nothing else."
-Sri Ramakrishna

103

Sally (Saturday, September 19, 2009 3:07 PM)

This is probably the perfect quote

Scott (Sunday, September 20, 2009 12:05 AM)

and one I need to think about daily, along with thoughts, such as:

"...The body was born and it will die. But for the soul there is no death... After realizing God one does not identify oneself any more with the body. Then one knows that body and soul are two different things."
-Sri Ramakrishna

There is the hint of an emerging Balmorhea State Park (with a little lake/natural springs diving for the "girls" scheduled in), to include Monahans Sand Hills State Park on the way, and then Big Bend afterward RV trip. I think it maps out to a pretty relaxed week long trip.....but along with Heidi and Devette [Heidi's co-scuba diving friend], I don't want to do it without you and Kel. I know you don't have any vacation left, but maybe we can work something out. I'll send you possible dates. The Balmorhea to Big Bend and back via Alpine and Marathon is all scenic drive. We could spend a night in Terlinqua (nothing for RV in Big Bend obviously) -in between two days in Big Bend (and maybe drink tequilla and listen to Jerry Jeff Walker).

Sally (Sunday, September 20, 2009 7:14 PM)

That is another great quote - maybe follows right after the first one? The RV trip sounds interesting - I never got to Balmorhea although I have passed it to get to Alpine and Ft Davis. Can't do it Oct 29-Nov 1 as I will be on a women's church retreat (called a "Walk to Emmaus" - learning about what it means to serve) and not at Thanksgiving since Mom & Dad will be there. But depending on the dates maybe we could do some or part of the trip. Also I just finished training to be a facilitator for Stephen Ministry Small Group supervision. We meet the 2nd & 4th Wednesdays, and I start as the facilitator for my own group Oct 14, so would like to try not missing a session. Let us know what dates you are looking at.

And remember that we were chosen by God and He is with us even to the end of the earth (or to the end of time as each "body" knows this earth & time, then we are with Him forever in another form/place/understanding).

Love - your sister

[We did take the above described RV trip, and it was fantastic. Regarding Sally's "Walk to Emmaus", see also the poem *To Serve* and corresponding notes].

—⟋⟋⟍—

Scott (Monday, September 21, 2009 1:58 AM)

Regarding progress on the first and initiated second novel, I'm still editing/writing the first novel, but i need to work harder on both..........as they are important statements (at least to me, even if no one reads them) regarding my past mental life and past/current/hopefully future spiritual realizations, respectively. Expressing them in an entertaining manner without over stating is the challenge, of course, especially for a science vs. fictional writer. I've been a little bogged down with thoughts of my disease as i feel my "good leg" progressing and thus am more aware of the steady deterioration and impending wheel chair future, etc.

I should thank God for this time to concentrate on the inside, but...it's not always so easy, at least for me (maybe others could handle it better?)

Anyway: Heidi is off tomorrow and Friday....which is our anniversary. She has been going "natural" (she can provide you with more details, I'm an innocent beneficiary of the good food), with wholesome real food, so she is also eating good meat of the unprocessed, free-range, etc. type [Heidi had been eating vegetarian]. She made awesome venison tenderloin medallions last night (from tenderloin/back straps of a deer that a friend had hunted... so not processed...and despite Heidi's anti-hunting attitude, as "already there" sort of thing) and has been making traditional foods at home, such as home made chicken stock and the beef-bone derived beef stock that has been simmering in the kitchen all day...driving me...and the dogs crazy...but i get pot-roast and the dogs get bones, respectively. Thought about going out for anniversary, but she mentioned making a rack of lamb so I thought I'd open a 1996 Ducru Beaucaillou that she bought me for an anniversary in Nashville. (I also have 2000 and 2003, monster vintages that will drink well if I make more anniversaries...)

So, in line with one of the potential themes of my "third" (second) book (it's a <u>Wilburys'</u> Thing....), if one ever develops AMONGST my late night drivel, but hopefully more in what I will pray to increasingly see in my meditations, even if in a darn wheel chair....

"Likewise, if God gives us this flash of divine light, all our doubts are destroyed. Can one ever know God by mere reasoning?"
-Sri Ramakrishna

love and peace, ss

Sally (Monday, September 21, 2009 10:31 AM)

Wow - lots of info [Much of the detail regarding a possible future novel was omitted from the above message during editing]. You have put a lot of thought into the 3rd book (got the Wilburys' thing) and it sounds interesting - Kel's genre for sure.

Another good quote - funny how "knowing" God is a heart/soul thing and not a head thing when "knowing" is usually the domain of the head/brain.

later - Sally

—⟶⟵—

Scott (Sunday, September 27, 2009 12:30 AM)

"The Lord has done so many things - will He not show people the way to worship Him? If they need teaching, then He will be the Teacher. He is our Inner Guide."
-Sri Ramakrishna

Sally (Sunday, September 27, 2009 11:11 PM)

Another really good quote - and He is our guide, just waiting till we come and say we are ready. He doesn't force the way. He isn't a puppet master pulling the strings but is the wise and knowledgeable guide when we are ready to be taught, to be led.

—⟶⟵—

Sally (Wednesday, September 30, 2009 12:59 AM)

Hey - where is my daily Ramakrishna?! Haven't gotten one in couple days...!

Scott (Wednesday, September 30, 2009)

You get a juicy one now:

The Master sings:

"Taking the name of Kāli, dive deep down, O mind,
Into the soul's fathomless sea;
But never believe the bed of the ocean bare of pearls

If in the first few dives you fail.
With firm resolve and self-control
Dive deep and make your way to Mother Kāli's realm.
Deep in the sea, O mind, of the Knowledge of Mother Kāli
Lie the lustrous pearls of peace;
If you but cherish love and follow the scripture's rule,
You can possess them for yourself.

But in those silent ocean depths
Six alligators lurk - lust, anger, and the rest -
Swimming about in search of prey.
Smear your body well with the turmeric of <u>viveka</u>;
The pungent smell of it will shield you from their touch."
- Sri Ramakrishna

Sally (Wednesday, September 30, 2009)

Wow - there's a lot here, needs to be studied as I'm not sure what it all means though I think I can follow some of it. Is Mother Kāli another aspect of God?

[See Glossary regarding "Kāli" and "Mother Kāli"]

—⟿—

Scott (Saturday, October 3, 2009 2:51 AM)

"You may speak of the scriptures, of philosophy, of Vedanta; but you will not find God in any of these. You will never succeed in realizing God unless your soul becomes restless for Him."
-Sri Ramakrishna

Sally (Sunday, October 4, 2009 12:41 AM)

Guess I need to read my Ramakrishna book - didn't you give me one for my birthday? The last several quotes you have sent have really been good and significant. This is kind of what my Christian meditation book is telling me also: that you can go through the motions of meditation but you aren't going to necessarily find God in those steps unless you are really open and awake and ready to be filled with God. God is always and already there but we are not always in the right "place" to receive him (nor are we capable of truly being in the moment, of sitting still and being deeply awake and yet also deeply restful - sitting still even if you feel a pain or itch or hear sounds).

Going to bed now to read some more - have Sunday school class on that book tomorrow.

Love and peace - your sister

Scott (Sunday, October 4, 2009 2:31 AM)

Yes. I gave you The Gospel of Ramakrishna (little hard bound book with pale yellowish cover). It is the most important book I believe I have ever read. [See Book List].

As I've noted before, Ramakrishna found samadhi (moksha/realization) through so many different paths. However, love of God was most important to him, and he believed in God as without form and God with form, perhaps irritating or at least confusing some of his Brāhmo Samāj colleagues and others who could only oversimplify their thoughts/religious approach by being only <u>dualists</u> or non-dualists. Yet some of these became his devotees when attempting to debate these various issues with him---which were basically non-issues to Ramakrishna.

In the Vedantic approach, one cannot come to realization without renunciation (related to your mediation comments). However, there is a different role/path for householders vs. <u>sannyasins</u> (monks). I would like to progress towards the latter stages of life as recognized in the classical Hindu system, which have been imposed upon me as much as a couple of decades "prematurely". Once one is done with his worldly duties, he can focus on realization/spiritual discipline, (the <u>vanaprastha</u>, or forest dweller, stage even if one didn't later go on to the sannyasin, or world renouncer/wandering ascetic stage).

As you will see when you read Ramakrishna, there is NOTHING BUT COMPATIBILITY with your Christian (true Christian) beliefs, and you will only find reinforcement for the teachings of Jesus amongst Ramakrishna's beautiful lessons of God-love. (You will also find him an adorable, almost goofy little pure spirit man...like a Yoda...small, eventually frail, and only concerned with love of God, and NEVER having uttered a single negative word towards anyone or anything).

I also believe, as Ramakrishna mentions in passing, that not all Vedantic studiers have to have a guru per se. It is classical Vedantic teaching that one must have a guru, but I don't have a guru. I wonder if I can dismiss this, but yet still believe all the rest. Ramakrishna did say it was possible, but required an exceptional person/spirit. (But this also may not apply as much to the Bhakti-Yoga as Jnana-Yoga path). My gut feeling is: ancients may have had access to portions of or all the Vedantic texts (not like in today's book distribution and market-place system), but without commentary/guidance, so they needed someone who had come to realization to help them understand the meanings. Current versions are all written with commentaries by the likes of Nikhilananda and other enlightened individuals, who in essence are our gurus, as spirits and by providing helpful guidance. Ramakrishna did say, in a quote I sent before, that God is our inner guide. So as I said, if a Guru showed up at my door tomorrow, I'd take him/her in, but otherwise, these great thinkers who have achieved moksha and samadhi and God realization and understand Brahman and the <u>Atman</u>, will be my gurus.

Now a quote...

"What is needed is absorption in God - loving Him intensely. The "Nectar Lake" is the Lake of Immortality. A man sinking in it does not die, but becomes immortal."
-Sri Ramakrishna

peace, ss

Sally (Sunday, October 4, 2009 9:51 PM)

Thanks for the info and I think you are correct - you don't need an actual guru, you have Ramakrishna and Vivekananda and God to be the guru. When I start reading the book, we will definitely talk about the book. Once again, another great saying - and goes hand in hand with the concept of meditation, immersing oneself in the meditation in order to be absorbed in God.

Thanks - too bad about the Cowboys, but I have a hard time caring about that and maybe so do you now.

Love and peace, your sister

Scott (Sunday, October 4, 2009 9:52 PM)

Watched the "game" and had dinner; and yes, football doesn't mean that much to me, anymore [I hope]. I watch and cheer, but the results are not key to any part of my true happiness. I just need my family, friends, animals (part of family), books, wine/food, closed eyes and a hopefully quiet or at least properly directed mind.

"The body has, indeed, only a momentary existence. God alone is real."
-Sri Ramakrishna

Sally (Monday, October 5, 2009 12:22 AM)

Your focus is right on - I know that it is hard to keep on that track, and the Ramakrishna quote (if I may be allowed a morbid moment) would be a perfect epitaph. I am trying to find balance in how I spend my time - wish my job didn't have to consume so much of my time, as well as my commute on office days, but I choose to live where I find happiness. I would much rather spend more time reading, talking with you, meditating (now that I have started that), and doing church volunteer work with the community here in Pueblo where I see so much need. Of course, I would also like to travel!

Off to bed to read, you can text if you want to chat more.

Love and peace, your sister

—⁂—

Scott (Tuesday, October 6, 2009 9:44 PM)

By the way, as per your text, our email correspondences are "our thing". I will try to leave Heidi a few notes, and I will write Travis some letters to parallel some financial leavings for certain milestones (MFA, marriage, kids, etc). I hope that I leave Heidi aspects of myself on a daily basis, without requiring anything more formal (other than "The Little Green Soul Book"). The emails between you and I are our shared thoughts, and if you want to, I encourage you to keep them. I don't think it will be one of those deals where I'm a famous posthumous author and you can publish our correspondences...sorry. But, this is a way we can communicate on a steady basis on the crucial things of life as we all carry on about our lives and after-lives....

Referring to Jnana-Yoga as well as Bhakti-Yoga...

"The path of knowledge leads to Truth, as does the path that combines knowledge and love. The path of love, too, leads to this goal."
-Sri Ramakrishna

I will try to find God through love, incorporating other paths as they occur to me, with my "inner" guide.

peace, ss

Sally (Wednesday, October 7, 2009)

I have a "Scott" folder on our email which is where I have been keeping the emails between you and me. I have also kept some of the texts you have sent me.

I wish now that I'd been writing them all down as I have limited space on the cell phone to save so maybe I will start a journal of the texts so I can delete and save space. But just about everything we have talked about and shared are things I want to save just because. I'm not going to get maudlin right now because I am tired and not looking forward to the rest of my work week and could start crying very easily and then won't sleep well and have to go to my office in Colo Springs the next 2 mornings, but you and I were on the same wave length about saving our text/email correspondences.

Your idea of leaving Heidi a few notes makes me think of the movie "PS I Love You" - part of me thinks that's a neat idea to come across notes some time later and then I'm not sure how someone would take that. But you're right about the other things on a daily basis. I do think Travis would appreciate the letters in reference to specific milestones.

Heading off to bed to read a little so I can drift off to sleep - was after midnight before I went to bed last night and can't do that when I have to get up at 5:00am! Getting tired of my government job! But at least I have a job.

Love and peace, your sister.

Scott (Tuesday, October 7, 2009)

We actually had re-watched "PS I Love You" the other night. I commented that that guy (it is a movie after all, so he had screenwriter help...) set the bar high! My notes to H will largely be within the little cheap green spiral notebook I had started to put various scriptures, lyrics, and quotes in, before I got any nicer journals for other things.

Here is the link to the meditation chairs we got; seagrass is a type of chair, with the back support, recommended by others seeking lumbar nurturing while soul searching, etc; likely on multiple sites, but not much price difference to my recollection, and I think this is where we ordered (I'm an electronic pack rat as well...):

[Link omitted during editing. Sally was having quite a bout of sciatica during all this time, and it still flairs. I certainly remember hoping despite the absence of classical pain and sensory abnormalities that my presenting symptoms of left hip flexor weakness and quadriceps atrophy could somehow be due to a nerve root problem...oh well...no one lives in the physical form forever].

Sally (Wednesday, October 7, 2009 6:55 PM)

Just ordered the seagrass meditation chair - natural wood stain and white unbleached cotton fabric. Thanks.

—⟋⟍—

Scott (Monday, October 12, 2009 2:35 AM)

"With a joyful face chant the sweet name of God,
Till, like a wind, it churns the nectar sea;
Drink of that nectar ceaselessly
(Drink it yourself and share it with all).
If ever your heart goes dry, repeat God's name.
(If it goes dry in the desert of this world,
Love of God will make it flow again).

...

Be watchful, that you may never forget to chant.
His mighty name: when danger stares in your face,
Pray to your Father Compassionate.
Snap sin's bonds with a shout of joy
(Crying, "To God, to God be the Victory!")
Come, let us be mad in the bliss of God,
Fulfilling all our hearts' desires,
And quench our thirst with the yoga of love."

-The young Narendra (eventually Swami Vivekananda), singing in the presence of The Master and other devotees

Sally (Monday, October 12, 2009 11:50 PM)

Thanks but you owe me a couple nights! Just cuz I wasn't here doesn't mean you shouldn't send them to me.

—⟋⟍—

Heidi (October 12, 2009) [Heidi sent us an astounding quote, which prompted a round of thought and commentary]

"A human being is part of the whole called by us universe, a part limited in time and space. We experience ourselves, our thoughts and feelings as something separate from the rest. A kind of optical delusion of consciousness. This delusion is a kind of prison for us, restricting us to our personal desires and to affection for a few persons nearest to us. Our task must be to free ourselves from the prison by widening our circle of compassion to embrace all living creatures and the whole of nature in its beauty. The true value of a human being is determined by the measure and the sense in which they have obtained liberation from the self. We shall require a substantially new manner of thinking if humanity is to survive."

- Albert Einstein, 1954

Scott (Monday, October 12, 2009 10:44 PM)

What a great quote! I can't imagine how any human could be as brilliant as he obviously was based on his insights (e.g. relativity theory, gravitational fields, quantum physics) into the true nature of things, taking the world so forward, conceptually and "functionally", and yet be so enlightened spiritually. I can't help but think that those two were related.

Where are these great thought and spiritual leaders NOW? We are SO off track as a species. I got distracted (but hopefully, with some good coming out of it) with my own little world of medical science and work ethic. I think I may have missed some of the "movements" I'm seeing evidence for now, but it still seems to me (in addition to less dramatic progress in theoretical physics), that the spiritual re-visitation movements are being more led/realized/searched for by frustrated non-scientist lay people, looking for true answers that haven't come in our technological world....not by science (largely a bunch of machines locked onto various modifications of the concrete one gene-one protein-one disease-one dissertation-one post doc-one grant world....) and certainly not by the Church (at least at the "global/leadership" level).

I sometimes (now) wonder if I should have taken a different approach, but I think my experience in that world, with a different mind set, and my relationships have put me exactly where I need to be...to hopefully come to some terms (wouldn't it be nice to have the time to try and "spread it") before I move on to that land where maybe someday my little spirit can hang with the likes of Jesus, Einstein, etc.

Thanks (hope you don't mind if i forward to Sally and Travis so they can see the quote)

Sally (Tuesday, October 13, 2009 11:32 AM)

I like the Einstein quote - don't know much about him, but he was right on target with that thinking. It seems like you can't get people to consider the humane aspects of something unless you make them feel it in relation to people closest to them. They lack a global concept of the connection of all human beings and all living things, yet we are all created by the same Creator with the same Love. Why do we have such animosity toward anything or anyone that is "different"? And why does it take something so large, so horrific, so "earth-shattering" as global wars or destruction to get our attention? I don't understand "man". I would like to think ethics has a bigger role in science and medicine.

—⟋⟍—

Scott (Wednesday, October 14, 2009 3:04 AM)

"I" and "mine" - that is ignorance. True knowledge makes one feel: "O God, You alone do everything. You alone are my own. And to You alone belong houses, buildings, family, relatives, friends, the whole world. All is Yours."
-Sri Ramakrishna

Sally (Wednesday, October 14, 2009 2:04 PM)

This is so very true - and no matter what we think about our achievements, we only have those things (house, car, family, other possessions) because of God and what He has done for us, what we are able to do through Him. We so very often forget to be thankful even for the little things. When I have spent several days with a bad headache or my leg hurting, I try to thank God when I notice I no longer have the pain. After reading books by Philip Yancy and Dr. Brand (who worked with lepers who have no sense of feeling/touch), I should also thank God that I can feel the pain I feel. When I get irritated about my job and wish I didn't have this job, I do make myself stop and thank God that I have a job, especially in today's world when so many don't have any work or the necessities of life that come from having a job. This is a good quote. Thanks.

Love and peace, your sister

Scott (Wednesday, October 14, 2009 7:10 PM)

I agree with your comments. This philosophy is also a way of approaching "detachment", which Ramakrishna also prescribed even in the context of Bhakti. This is hard; meaning you shouldn't value your possessions (not that difficult, per se), but implying that you shouldn't love your wife or kids in any special manner other than as parts of the unity of all things is harder. I suppose this is the sort of Buddhist approach to oneness that thus helps alleviate suffering. But I'm not sure I buy into this. I certainly believe in the oneness of all things. In part, this is supported by the lessons of particles physics, but conventional science is yet inadequate to explain things upward from there. Everything except our limited sense perceptions points to this, and it "feels" right. However, I don't necessarily *a priori* believe that suffering is to be avoided....at the expense of not feeling anything regarding special relationships.

I may love millions of different people if I had encountered them in the same way that I have you, or Heidi, or Travis, etc.....and I hope that we can all treat non-immediate family with the same love and respect; but, there are bonds that develop between people who are together...kindred spirits. And I don't think it is necessarily correct to run away from these or denounce them just to "alleviate suffering" (I'm sure I'm oversimplifying the Buddhist and Jnana-Yoga Vedantic approach in this regard.) But if we can recognize our personal loves in the context of divine love, the divinity of the soul, God as the "sum of all souls", it may not only make transitions easier, but increase appreciation while we're here. I think that what works for a monk living amongst other monks doesn't necessarily translate so easily to "householders", who marry, raise children, have to work, etc.

The Hindu stages of life (probably adhered to more in the past) certainly account for this. Earlier than expected due to terminal illness (but not that much younger than traditional Hindus reached it anyway), I now am in the vanaprastha analogous stage (and pondering full entry into sannyasin stage). So, none of that philosophy said it was bad to work (with right attitude toward end points...), to have possessions, etc. There were even formulas for how much should be spent on material things, charity, etc....but then you reach a point where you then visit/re-visit the true meaning of life, progressing towards recognizing the Atman, the Soul or the Self, as One with Brahman, the Absolute.

I think there's a "middle ground": we see all the universe as one; that which makes it so will also help us deal with "loss", put things in proper context, and the love that develops between people can only help the "oneness" by spreading it in everything we do everyday. There are no words to express how sad I would be if I lost Heidi, Travis, you, (and although expected, to someday lose Mom and Dad). I do not care to avoid that suffering at the expense of all the love it helped me realize along the way. I do not believe that life is supposed to be physically and emotionally pain free. I believe spiritual knowledge helps us to understand it, live through it, live correctly, and live in some form forever.

But....somehow I was the coward, as it looks like I'm going to check out first...maybe dying is the easy part and living on after loss is harder. Although the dying part is sometimes pretty scary...

more Ramakrishna to come

OM

Sally (Thursday, October 15, 2009 12:05 AM)

Wow - there is a lot here to address. I agree with you that there has to be some "middle ground" regarding certain love/attachment relationships. I know in the Greek language there are several words for love that distinguish love we feel for spouse/child/parent vs. for fellow human, and as you and I discussed in a prior email, if there could be more of the fellow human being love (which too many people misunderstand – "ooh I can't 'love' that person, I don't even know him/her" or "but that person is Oriental and I'm Hispanic, I can't 'love' them", etc) there would be so much less anger and hate and fighting - except for the real fanatic for which there may be no answer, but I don't think they are the majority. But if we have the agape love (I think that's the fellow human being love) for others as well as the close relationship love, it should be OK to have the close relationship love.

The attachment to "things" is just ridiculous, and I have been guilty of that myself. Like when Kel and I got flooded [when living north of Houston] by Tropical Storm Allison and had the house damage and lost things and our lives were unsettled for several months. There was definitely a time of stress (that was one of the big stressors in our lives in the last 10+ years). We lost some clothes, bedding, books, had some furniture affected and had to have the house repaired - insurance covered that, and we were inconvenienced. But that was all. It's just things and if we didn't buy so many things, we wouldn't get so upset at the loss of things. And we'd have more money to help with more important issues like world poverty and hunger and endangered animals. But I don't think there is any way to completely avoid suffering and I know the Bible mentions that there will always be suffering - God is here to help us get through that, and I think we are supposed to help others through their suffering, and we are not supposed to add to anyone's suffering.

Unfortunately greed-hungry people don't stop to think about others' suffering or their impact on other people - that's where the need for a global outlook comes from that I mentioned in the earlier email. Without the global outlook or concern, some people can only see themselves and their place in the world and work to achieve their desires without concern for their fellow human beings, when with just a small effort on everyone's part we could take better care of more people's needs.

I don't think dying is the easy part, and I don't think living on is necessarily easier or harder. It all depends on what each of us brings to that perspective. We will all face challenges when we lose each one of our loved ones and when we face our end as well. But God is with us and hopefully each of us will have some loved one left to be with us. I wonder about that for myself, as I have no children - I do have 2 step-children, but I wonder where they will be when my time comes to die. Nobody should be alone at that time, and you most certainly will not be.

As far as avoiding the suffering: I think about people who are afraid of the loss, so they don't take the chance, and what they have missed in their lives. If Kel dies before me, I will likely not marry again, but I am so very happy that I found him and have had so many years with him and wouldn't have missed any of the years. The suffering of loss does hurt, but to miss what preceded the loss would make for a lonely, sad life, and God made us to be happy people.

Love and peace, your sister

Scott (Thursday, October 15, 2009 2:50 AM)

Thanks for all your comments. I strongly doubt you have to worry too much about dying alone...and I also think you have many years left with Kel. But, as follow up to the sentiment of yesterday's quote:

"Therefore a man should act in such a way that he may have bhakti at God's Lotus Feet and love God as his very own. You see this world around you. It exists for you only for a couple of days. There is nothing to it."
-Sri Ramakrishna

Sally (Thursday, October 15, 2009 9:50 AM)

Thanks. I like this - this world is but a temporary repose and our true home is waiting for us with God.

—⁓—

Scott (Friday, October 16, 2009 2:08 AM)

"It is true that one or two can get rid of the "I" through samadhi; but these cases are very rare. ...Therefore if the "I" must remain, let the rascal remain as the "servant I."
-Sri Ramakrishna

Sally (Friday, October 16, 2009 1:23 PM)

We can learn to stop saying "I have this" and "I own that" and "I am better than this person", etc. But when expressing love or sympathy or sorrow, it is difficult to keep out the word "I" if one wants to make it personal; e.g., "I'm sorry for your loss", "I love you", "I am so happy for you", etc unless you are able to express the emotion for more than one person; e.g., "we are happy for you", "we are sorry for your loss". But love is very personal and usually expressed one-on-one and it's difficult to get the "I" out of "one". Of course, I know Ramakrishna was trying to get the focus of love on a more global scale and less on the intimate personal relationship scale.

Scott (Friday, October 16, 2009 9:11 PM)

I think that is exactly what is meant by the "servant I"; that God is the object of your love and the doer of all things, and the "I" that remains is recognizing that he is the doer and that "I" is not bad. This is the Bhakti-Yoga approach. I also think this fits in nicely with psychological approaches such as Jung's feeling that the first part of life is for developing an adequate sense of ego, in order to function and then later, more fully develop the Self.

So for those who can't ignore the world and reality, loving from a personal perspective is fine when that "I" is the "servant of God" and we do things through that benevolent sense of oneness. Despite my often rational self (which with a bigger dose of discipline could in theory facilitate Raja-Yoga), my logical and analytical makeup supporting an "awareness" of oneness [still more intellectually approached than directly experienced] (which could underlie a Jnana-Yoga approach), and the ethically valid work I've done in the past (related perhaps to the aspirations of Karma-Yoga), I believe passionate love for God could have the most appeal to me right now; that is, Bhakti-Yoga.

Especially later in his life (particularly after he developed cancer), Ramakrishna saw God with attributes (particularly in other beings) as well as without attributes. I believe lovers of fellow men and nature, etc are more likely to be Bhakti-Yogis and see beauty and God in all things, especially other humans. [Realized Jnana-Yogis see everything as one, and hence all aspects of the created world as manifestations of the one Divine Consciousness].

Maybe a little bit of all these paths may make sense, as in a combination of spiritual aspirations, and it may be possible at least to appreciate these different paths to God. Swami Vivekananda expressed that a man who could manifest aspects of all four yogas is the best ideal man [and indicated that the different yogas support each other.]

So, when you say "I am sorry for your loss" that is the good residual "I" of the God-loving and serving Bhakta; not the "I" of "I want a Ferrari so I can get laid despite my absolute lack of any real spiritual substance." (In other words, we can't all be Buddha or The Dali Lama, and our lives have different human love personal aspects, and that is NOT a bad thing, as we discussed in last emails).

According to the Master, then:

> **"...The bhakta keeps this "I-consciousness". He says, "O God, Thou art the Master and I am Thy servant", ...His "I" is not completely effaced. Again, by constantly practicing this kind of "I-consciousness", one ultimately attains God. This is called bhaktiyoga."**
> -Sri Ramakrishna

and since I owed you a couple from the past, in support of all this:

> **"A man becomes liberated even in this life when he knows that God is the doer of all things."**
> -Sri Ramakrishna

> **"Bhakti, love of God, is the essence of all spiritual discipline. Through love one acquires renunciation and discrimination naturally."**
> -Sri Ramakrishna

peace, ss

Sally (Saturday, October 17, 2009 12:53 AM)

Thanks for the extra Ramakrishna quotes tonight. I like the last 2. Fits in with the Christian meditation class I am taking for Sunday school.

My meditation chair comes tomorrow. Their warehouse is here in Colorado and their email to me said they'll be in the Pueblo area Saturday. So part of my housework tomorrow will be to set up the meditation area downstairs. I put my incense down there. I will take down all the appropriate CD's and set up some candles. My Sunday School meditation book even suggested a sort of altar area with things that are meaningful; for some people a cross or a sacred image, like what you have set up with your statues and prints and artwork.

Peace and love, your sister

Scott (Sunday, October 18, 2009 1:02 AM)

I'm no expert on what a meditation altar should include. As you know as well as I do, many different things can support or facilitate meditation. Some of these descend to us from The Yoga Sutra of Patanjali, which I've read parts of. As it is an extremely objective approach to what I see as a parallel to the pathway of Raja (Concentration) Yoga, I anticipate revisiting the rest of the text soon. Many suggestions are offered, and he recommends only focusing on one (or one at a time). Yet, I sometimes find myself (especially when japa and divine cravings don't seem to be getting me anywhere as my cerebral nightmare races...) giving a go at multiple approaches.

My last twenty five years have almost made me the "anti-meditation", which is probably why I try so hard to read things now that are so different than in the past. So take my advice with a grain of salt (but, certainly not that of Patanjali or The Dali Lama): one useful thing is to focus on an object that HAS NO VALUE to you, per se (of course, we should have no attachments to anything...as we've discussed).

I find the Shiva Nataraja (Dancing Shiva) statuette useful in this exercise. Yes, it has some attributes that could have given it value in the past, such as: I gave it to Heidi for her birthday (about 1 month into my ALS diagnosis) and I think it's beautiful, etc.; but, I try to approach it objectively. His right hand holds the drum of creation; the left hand the fire of destruction (how can anything like the cycle of creation and destruction be more objective and non-"personally" meaningful); the other right hand is held up to give us a sign of peace and tell us to relax about this inevitability; the other left hand is held above and indicating one lifting leg as a symbol of stepping over or elevating above Maya; and the other leg is stomping on a demon, as a symbol of ignorance. Nothing could be so instructive to the soul.

So, when I need to concentrate on something that is neutral, I find myself staring at the chest of the Nataraja, the perfectly level pathway between creation (what I and so many have undergone in this physical universe) and destruction (which I am on an accelerated course for, but which everyone else is inevitably progressing towards). I have also seen highly radiant (even blurred at the edges) images of a cross when I mediate. I would not fault anyone with this [a cross] as a centerpiece on their mediation table that's for sure.

So, when at least attempting to meditate, I also take note of my surroundings, as one of the meditation guides that Heidi gave me early on with my Mala beads suggested this as an early step. I was initially adverse to emphasis on breathing (prevalent in meditation guides), as I knew this was the aspect of my form that would likely kill me with ALS, but this has gotten less scary lately. So this is an approach as well, as you know.

Heidi is much more knowledgeable about good sources of the juicy incense stuff, and we'll score you some of that really thick, long burning, uber fragrance emanating sandalwood stuff she gets me, and which I use when I anticipate, or hope for, one of those really long conversations with God

peace, ss

[I must try to work harder on my meditating. In addition to use of musical CDs, without breathing instructions, Katy Rigler gave me a CD with natural sounds that are supposed to stimulate alpha and theta waves in the brain, associated with deep relaxation and concentration.]

Sally (Sunday, October 18, 2009 9:00 AM)

Good night! but you do put a lot of thought and work into your replies! But that's OK, it looks like some of my [long and detailed] work histories. Thanks for the meditation info and altar info; works right into my meditation book for my Sunday School class. I do plan to set up a site, as I do know I will need help with focus. I want to spend time on meditation, but am still struggling with the idea of what else I "should" be spending my time doing. By going to a dedicated site to do the meditation, I am away from the convenience of doing housework and will be better able to only concentrate on meditation.

More later - Kel just made hotcakes for breakfast (do still need to think about feeding the body).

Love and peace - your sister

—✄—

Sally (Monday, October 19, 2009 11:05 AM)

Dude: where is my Ramakrishna?

Scott (Friday, October 23, 2009 3:24 AM)

"He had found that the one idea in all religions is, "not me, but Thou", and he who says, "not me", the Lord fills his heart. The less of this little "I" the more of God there is in him."
-Swami Vivekananda

[At this point, began adding quotes from Swami Vivekananda, Ramakrishna's disciple].

Sally (Friday, October 23, 2009 11:25 AM)

The plants have been perishing without their daily water! Thank you for bringing back the water. This is such a simple concept, but so true. You cannot be filled with "I" and still have room for God, and since "I" cannot do what one needs in life, one should get rid of as much of it as possible and look to God for the rest. The life filled with "I" is usually shallow and unsatisfying if one really looks close enough at it and is honest enough about it.

Thank you, and don't you think you should send me a few more to make up for the several days that were barren?

Mom and Dad really enjoyed their time with you all and really enjoyed their meals!

Peace & love - your sister

Scott (Saturday, October 24, 2009 1:09 AM)

Vivekananda on Religion:

-**"There never was my religion or yours, my national religion or your national religion; there never existed many religions, there is only the one. One Infinite Religion existed all through eternity and will ever exist, and this Religion is expressing itself in various countries, in various ways."**

-**"I do not understand how people declare themselves to be believers in God, and at the same time think that God has handed over to a little body of men all truth, and they are the guardians of the rest of humanity."**

-**"Man is to become divine by realising the divine; idols or temples or churches or books are only the supports, the helps, of his spiritual childhood: but on and on he must progress."**

-**"Love and charity for the whole human race, that is the test of true religiousness."**

-**Swami Vivekananda**

Sally (Saturday, October 24, 2009 1:13 PM)

Thanks - I especially like the last 2, most particularly the last one.

—⁊⁊⁊—

Scott (Tuesday, October 27, 2009 2:38 AM)

On Atman or the Self:

"That very thing which we now see as the universe, will appear to us as God (Absolute), and that very God who has so long been external will appear to be internal, as our own Self."

"Satisfy yourself once that you are the infinite spirit. If that is true, it must be nonsense that you are the body. You are the Self, and that must be realised. Spirit must see itself as spirit."
-Swami Vivekananda

Sally (Tuesday, October 27, 2009 10:27 AM)

I especially like the 2nd. We are what is encased in the body: our soul or Self or spirit, which is one with God. It is only housed in the body to exist for a while here on earth, but the body won't be needed later. Thanks

―☋―

Scott (Wednesday, October 28, 2009 12:44 AM)

re. Bhakti-Yoga:

"Bhakti-Yoga is a real, genuine search after the Lord, a search beginning, continuing and ending in Love. One single moment of the madness of extreme love to God brings us eternal freedom."
-Swami Vivekananda

Sally (Wednesday, October 28, 2009)

Thanks for this one. I really need to make time in my day - take time in my day - for my meditation on a regular basis. It is wrong to give everything else in my life some form of priority over spending at least a few minutes in contemplation on God, loving God through searching for him in prayer and mediation. None of the other things in my day are more important yet I find time for them.

I am heading out tomorrow evening through Sunday afternoon on a church women's retreat called a "Walk to Emmaus". It has to do with service - service to God; learning to serve as Jesus served (comes from a story in the Bible in which the disciples didn't recognize Jesus at the seashore and still He cooked and served them fish, and they knew Him in His service to them...something on those lines). Anyway there will be Bible reading and prayer and meditation - no Facebook or TV or cell phones, etc - and no housework! I'm almost scared to think about what this house will look like with me gone and Kel and Rocket [Sally's very attached female German Shepherd] in charge!

I love you and I love how you are caring for yourself with your reading and how you are sharing that with us. I really appreciate it and I feel I have benefitted greatly from your sharing.

Peace and love, your sister

Scott (Wednesday, October 28, 2009)

I understand your comments about taking time out for meditation. Even with my now open schedule, I sometimes don't. I think I may sometimes avoid it because of how scary some of the topics are, but skipping is not good for me.

The last two or three days I have been particularly depressed and anxious about my ALS, and what is coming. The objective weakening of my legs is a tangible parameter.

I had recently read a book by William Styron [See Book List] that was a memoir of his experience with his severe depression (from which I believe he "recovered"). It was masterfully written. I would expect it could be quite harrowing to those experiencing similar feelings. In no disrespect to severe so-called primary depression, for which most patients can expect improvement and bounce back, I began thinking of the particular dread of being saddened to similar levels of despair, but by a different underlying cause: the prospect of an irreversible, terminal disease, particularly one with an unpleasant progression.

As you've said, I should let any poetic thoughts come out. So, wrote a moderately long poem last night (7 stanzas with 8 lines per stanza, and with rhymes or near rhymes). I thought about not sharing it....as it is dark, with frank comments on the justification for suicide; a flat out "Fuck Him" related to God, if he could dish out such pain and not allow relief; the nature of holding on for other's sake, etc. I just had been feeling palpably gloomy, and I thought that perhaps by facing my angst, my despair, my upcoming losses, it could be helpful...and then I meditated...and I will meditate again tonight. It is not good for me to not use that which could give me supporting strength.

I'll attach the first draft for you to have a look. It will need some editing if I revisit it; not sure I even want to (unless it is regarded as "expressive" and then only as "art" - at which point, I may take out the "Fuck Him" part, and already told God I was doing it from the artist perspective addressing the bottom of my anguish---I need all the Divine help I can get!!!). But it is at least an attempt to communicate a level of despair that I can see occasionally too often now........ that I could never have imagined before this, and which I suspect some others have faced.

Your weekend of prayer and meditation and stepping back from the meaningless world sounds very rewarding. Do NOT worry about the house...or anything else

love, ss

[The comments above relate to the poem "Incurable Blues", included in this collection within the Darkness section].

124

Sally (Thursday, October 29, 2009 10:22 AM)

I'm not as worried about your despair as I used to be. Your readings and meditation have helped you a lot. And the writing - even if it's dark - is a great outlet/release, very therapeutic and cleansing. And it's OK to feel anger at God sometimes and to express it. He is big enough to handle that and loving enough to hold you in His arms while you are lashing out, just as any loving parent would do with a child who is upset and crying and flailing in the parent's arms. As long as you remember that God didn't "do" this to you and that He isn't a puppet master who pulls strings to allow or disallow things to happen. His role is to be with you, walk with you, love and guide and strengthen you until you get Home.

I am printing out the poem and will read it with the understanding that you had feelings that you needed to express and I will not worry about you. You are a much stronger person than you realize and I am very proud of you and love you more than you can understand, even if that isn't what Ramakrishna or Vivekananda recommends. But I love you not just because you are my brother, but also because you are a person that I believe is worthy of love and respect for your work and your ethics and your principles and your generosity - you have a very good heart and soul. Keep up with your meditation - and try to look at the "scary" topics objectively as if they belonged to someone else - they are just there. The Christian meditation book I am reading says we should neither accept nor reject those topics that come to us while we are trying to meditate. Let them float on by like barges on a canal; you merely notice them, without any real ownership or involvement. If you find yourself getting involved (climbing on board the barges), you retreat to your mantra and keep repeating it so that your mind cannot be preoccupied with the "barges".

I will not be able to share thoughts about the poem probably till Sunday evening. Feel free to call/email Kel, as he will want/need the company. He had a difficult night two nights ago with asthma and may not do well with me gone.

Peace and love and lots of prayers - your sister

—◆—

Sally (Monday, November 2, 2009 11:21 PM)

My dear dear brother:

Thank you for the wonderful letter and poem [for Sally's "Walk to Emmaus"; see poem notes]. You cannot imagine my surprise and honor and joy, when we got to the point in our program on Sunday in which they gave us our packages of information that also included letters/notes of encouragement and love and blessings from our retreat leaders and friends and family, and I found yours in there. Your words were very inspirational and part of the "icing on the cake" for what turned out to be a most wonderful renewal weekend that I wish everyone could enjoy. I know not everyone would come away with the same experience, but I truly felt and experienced the love of Christ surrounded by such wonderful sisters of faith and spending time in such a wonderful place in the mountains. (We had bad weather Thursday night that just kept getting better until Sunday, when the sun was actually warm and the skies were so blue. The pine trees were dusted with snow and with the view down into the valley, the entire place said "look at what the Lord has made!"). During our weekend, especially in our small groups, we all shared with each other things that touched our hearts, challenges in our lives, and places in our personal world where there was special hurting. Special prayers were said within the small groups. Within the entire program, special prayers were said if requests were forwarded (I sent a special prayer request for you) and we had people praying for our retreat the entire weekend.

I hope you can feel and understand how powerful a tool prayer is - even if it's just to bring some peace and calm to some fear or dark place. After this weekend I know that there is some mission meant for me but that right now the mission for me is to be with you whenever possible, to spend time with you and share my faith and whatever strength and calm I can pass on to you and to make sure you know how much you are loved and cared for and will be ongoing. If you have a need that I can take care of - I am here for you.

Love and peace and all my prayers, Sally

—॒॒॒—

Scott (Tuesday, November 3, 2009 10:35 PM)

"If you know that you are positively other than your body, you have then none to fight with or struggle against; you are dead to all ideals of selfishness. So the Bhakta declares that we have to hold ourselves as if we are altogether dead to all the things of the world; and that is indeed self-surrender. Let things come as they may. This is the meaning of "Thy will be done; ..."
-Swami Vivekananda

(this one hits a bit close to "home" these days....)

peace, ss

Sally (Wednesday, November 4, 2009 10:58 AM)

This is so very personal for you right now, but I have heard and I believe (as I have only experienced it on much more minor issues like my cancer scare years ago) that there is great peace when you can truly surrender all to God, give all your cares fully to Him. Let Him do all the worrying and you do all the worshiping - it's an uneven distribution of the workload, God getting the larger end of the load, but that's the way He prefers it. In our retreat this past weekend, we celebrated communion every day; and in one of the communions we first gave a symbolic offering of our burdens to God (piece of bread torn off, placed in a basket, basket placed at foot of cross in the chapel after all had done so) before we partook of communion. It was very moving and peaceful; if we can just remember to actually do that in our lives through our prayers and meditation. We don't have to be in charge or in control. We don't have to do it alone/go the journey alone. God is there for us always, even before we were born, and He walks with us and wants to be our comfort. We just need to come to Him, through prayer, through meditation, through surrender of our attempts at control, and through surrender of our cares and burdens.

Try this exercise when you are meditating: start out sitting tense physically and as you begin to meditate/pray/talk to God, begin to release the tension starting at the top of your body and working down to your legs/feet (especially since that is where your ALS is most apparent). Give your tension/your burden/ your cares over to God in prayer and meditation.

Thanks for resuming our daily journaling! Bless you. Love and peace and prayers, Sally

—◊—

Scott (Friday, November 6, 2009 1:59 AM)

Again, regarding Bhakti (Love of God):

"The true Bhakta's love is this burning madness, before which everything else vanishes for him. The whole universe is to him full of love and love alone; ...So when a man has this love in him, he becomes eternally blessed, eternally happy; the blessed madness of divine love alone can cure for ever the disease of the world that is in us."
-Swami Vivekananda

Sally (Friday, November 6, 2009 1:20 PM)

True and comforting. We were just discussing a somewhat similar idea or feeling in my office yesterday, when we were talking about how scary things are right now in our world, even in our country as far as the economy and politics. If you allow yourself to dwell on those issues and worry (which one would because things are very worrisome especially for the younger generations coming along), you could start to really panic and pile on the stress. But we were consciously deciding we weren't going to do that because we had God and His love to fall back on. We plan to think about and concentrate on one day at a time and dwell on thoughts of God's love and the knowledge and comfort of our long-term "future".

Thanks. Love and peace and prayers, Sally

Scott (Friday, November 6, 2009 2:31 PM)

All true. I've been doing some psych-related reading as related to topics touched on in Doris Lessing's *Briefing for a Descent Into Hell* [See Book List], and the messages are maybe even more appropriate for today. Firstly, what seems insane (as in people going through inner journeys) may actually be a more sensitive/spiritual approach or response to the insanity that is everywhere around us. Humans are extraordinarily alienated from themselves. The focus of most people (including for me for large parts of my life) is WAY off track for our mutual survival. With the last couple of shootings (Ft. Hood, Orlando) [see below*], it makes me ponder the accuracy of things I used to say: that people were no different today than in past, the main difference was access to firearms, so the key was to get rid of guns (which will never happen); that in the old days, if someone had a psychotic break and went crazy in the market place, the worst that would happen is that he'd club a couple of people before they would tackle and control him, and the problem now is that a student or Army Psychiatrist, etc can go into an open place and shoot 10 or 20 or 30 or 40 people before anything can be done. But, I am now suspecting that it isn't just the weapons; people are increasingly alienated. Anyone who can "adjust" to what we have generated as a society is in fact probably ill and doing the best they can to function at the ego level. How can we believe that this world we live in is "normal", with governments that can sanction the killing of more than 100,000,000 people alone in the last century? How can we "blame" anyone who freaks out and acts out?

I personally believe it is too late for mankind as a species. Maybe it was never intended for this world to be some great place. All anyone can do is be responsible for their own soul and their own actions. If this can spread to others, that is a great thing; but it is unlikely to spread to all six billion people, especially the ego-driven, psychopaths that are in charge and could care less about humanity.

If we really wanted to fix things here and now (i.e., vs. a future spiritual life), we'd have to strip it all down and start all over with completely different focus, and that will NEVER happen (unless we have a total nuclear holocaust and the only 50 survivors are a hidden Buddhist monastery...and a couple women working there for eventual reproduction).

No wonder so many poets and artists went "insane" and/or killed themselves. Anyone who can look into this situation with insight and sensitivity is saddened beyond hope, and yes, turning to God (and acting truly towards others in that spirit) is all one can do. Unfortunately for the species, that is a growing minority. We need the spirituality of the masses to change, so they can have (put in place) leaders who truly care about people...

oh well.....

[* Refers to the Fort Hood shooting on November 5, 2009, in which 13 people were killed and 30 others wounded. The accused shooter, Nidal Malik Hasan, is an American born Muslim, psychiatrist, and Major in the U.S. Army; and to the episode on November 6, 2009 in Orlando, FL where a man killed one person and injured another 5 in a shooting at the offices of an engineering firm from which the accused had been let go in 2007.]

Sally (Friday, November 6, 2009 4:59 PM)

That is part of the purpose of the "Walk to Emmaus" retreats. With so many churches dying out because their status quo no longer meets the needs of people today, there needs to be a reaching out and renewal to touch people - get more spirit filled people who feel a commitment and who then feel the mission to go back and help spread that to others around them. If we get more people to go on retreat, it hopefully helps attract more people into a church that has a new focus that speaks to the true needs of people, and more spreading and so on, and so on, etc. like a pebble tossed out into a lake that causes ripples. We can affect people by affecting those around us positively and then they affect others positively. Unfortunately the powers that be in our government leadership may not be within reach of the ripples and they are becoming increasingly less humanity-centered and more "I"-centered and power driven and "in-your-life control" driven. But then it has been predicted for several decades that the US would become a 3rd world country, and maybe that's the way it needs to be - the all powerful "I" world stripped down and sent back to simpler times.

Would love to take this up for further discussion on the RV trip.

Love and peace and prayers daily, Sally

—◈—

Scott (Saturday, November 7, 2009 12:25 AM)

I like Vivekananda's comments that the ideal person has some features or fully developed aspects of all four of the yogas. Although maybe tainted sometimes by pride and vanity, I feel that maybe I've done a decent job in the past of serving through work, and continue to do a little. I can't do the physical aspects of Raja-Yoga much, but do try to incorporate some concentration strategies...so MUCH to improve on though. The concepts of Jnana-Yoga "make sense" to me, including in the context of what we have gleaned from science, but I do not know "it"...because "it" is impossible to know...and I have to catch myself if I think I know "it". But, Vivekananda did stress that religion should make sense and should not be contradictory to our understanding or even to science--a modern take on Vedantic thought I suppose. I believe the principles of Jnana-Yoga, but this is the hardest approach, and the goal of Self-realization is essentially beyond man's mind...ANY man's mind; and I believe that the revealed truths in the Upanishads must be directly experienced. So, maybe by a combination of all paths I'll get an at least standing room only ticket in the after-life and won't have to spend too much time coming back to haunt anyone from Purgatory (or come back to Earth as one of those spider mites pestering my Fukien Tea bonsai....)

So, in support of Jnana-Yoga, on with some comments on Brahman, striking a bit of a "personal" chord:

"...hard hit by sorrows and afflictions, the eye will turn of itself to one's own real nature, the Inner Self. It is owing to the presence of this desire for bliss in the heart, that man, getting hard shocks, one after another, turns his eye inwards--to his own Self."
-Swami Vivekananda

peace, ss

Sally (Saturday, November 7, 2009 12:10 PM)

Such a true statement. And so many times, people who believe in God, especially Christians, have a tendency to think that life will be problem free because they believe in or follow God. Yet the Bible tells us in several places that there will be trials, that there is no perfect life for us here on earth (which is really only a temporary home). We must learn and remember to rely on, fall back on, lean on, trust in God and He will walk with us and help us through the trials.

130

We are not alone through the struggles. So why, when the troubles come, do we instantly think that God has abandoned us and wonder what we have "done wrong" to deserve this difficulty, this punishment. We must learn to see that it is NOT a punishment, that we do NOT deserve this, that God did NOT send it to us for sins we committed or sins of the fathers; those have all been washed away and forgiven. We live in a world that is plagued and diseased and imperfect and, like your beloved Bonsai pestered by mites, full of things that our fragile imperfect human bodies are unable to resist. But as humans, we say "why me?" and lose the global perspective or our sight on God and see (at least for awhile, though some may be unable to change even later) only the small self view.

But you have done well with turning and continuing to work to turn your Self eye back outward to God and to others. Not having read the books yet, I'm not sure which Yoga that is - but I will read and learn all that. Just the fact that you recognize the difference and want to read to learn and work on it means that you care about it. Deep down you were never a selfish person and have always had a generous heart and soul.

Thanks for sharing Vivekananda

Love and peace and prayers, Sally

Scott (Sunday, November 8, 2009 12:27 AM)

Thanks for your comments. I do get sad, periodically through the day, or get a sense of dread for what is coming. I hope I am spiritually "arming" myself, not just to deal with disease, but for what will come to face us all someday. I think the weakness scares me the most...maybe more than dying...but neither is particularly welcome at 46...soon to be 47!!!!!!!!!!! Although as Heidi says, so much of me is and always will be 12...but the more I read in religion and psychology, that may not be such a bad thing.

I agree with your comments, but somehow (despite the fact that I've always felt like God doesn't "micromanage" humans or the Earth)---that this (as in ALS) is "for a purpose". That may be just a defense mechanism, so to speak, or something I put in my conscious mind to make everything just a bit more barely endurable. But even if not for me specifically in the: "boy Scott, you've got some potential, but time to re-shift the focus", then at least in the context of what a hopefully strong soul/spirit can recognize in certain physical conditions.

Either way, I will hold on to the former "for a purpose" idea for a while, and try to carry on. I used to think that ALS was the worst thing that could happen to someone. A lot of that may have been induced by my med school recollections, some pop-culture dread, etc, and even an old friend sent a card stating basically that I "had received the worst hand possible." However, I've been very functional and remain moderately so... for the things that are important to me... for over six months already...and I suspect it could continue for a while yet...and we adjust one day or even one moment at a time. Years ago, I would have FREAKED OUT (and still do a bit) if I had woken up and couldn't lift my left toes or now left foot at all, but now I guess I'm thankful that I can still move my arms enough to move my left leg manually, and that it hasn't affected my swallowing (that is clear....I'm getting FAT!) or speech or breathing yet (although I sometimes imagine it is...). I guess I'll adjust gradually to other aspects of progression.

I try to not BE my disease when meditating. As I've said before, it made it possible by "forcing" me to reflect on my Self, etc....but, it is never too far from my mind and hard to make one of those barges floating down the river....

love, ss

Sally (Monday, November 9, 2009 1:03 AM)

Just a quick comment on your thought about the ALS maybe coming to you perhaps "for a purpose": Just because God likely didn't "give" ALS to you doesn't mean that He might not have "allowed" it to happen to you for a reason. We all know (those of us that believe in God and in God's ultimate ability) that God can reach down and cause things to happen or stop things from happening; there have truly been miracles. But sometimes He does allow things to happen for a reason, and perhaps in your case He did do just that because there is something you are meant to do, there is some duty you have, some good you are to perform, some task God has for you that can best be done with the ALS or the person you have become or are becoming as a result of the ALS.

And I think it is OK to have so much of you still be 12! The young people at our church seem to be able to relate to me and share with me to the point that I don't think they know how old I really am - but that's OK. I really enjoy talking with them and seeing what their world is like and that they feel comfortable enough with me to talk to me like that - but I sure wouldn't want to really be that age again right now!

As far as being your disease when meditating: try hard to just BE when meditating. You are not anything but a soul questing for God. Your ALS is just one aspect of you (you're a man, you're a doctor, you're married, you have a son, you have ALS, you're in your 40's...). You have thoughts about all these things, but when meditating you just note or acknowledge "yes" to the thoughts and focus back on the meditation. That's when you restate your mantra with a little more exertion to regain your focus. This is my mantra (I use it with my Mala beads or just regular meditation or centering prayer): "God almighty, Lord of Heaven, heal us with your love." It's just the right amount of syllables for me to capture my thoughts and concentration. If I need anything shorter, I just use "God almighty."

More later - Love and peace and prayers, Sally

—ɯ—

Scott (Sunday, November 15, 2009 2:59 AM)

"There is no limit to the power of the human mind. The more concentrated it is, the more power is brought to bear on one point; that is the secret."
-Swami Vivekananda

"The mind takes up various objects, runs into all sorts of things. That is the lower state. There is a higher state of the mind, when it takes up one subject, and excludes all others, of which samadhi is the result."
-Swami Vivekananda

Sally (Sunday, November 15, 2009 1:00 PM)

Because of the power of the mind, we need to work to direct our thoughts and concentration in the correct direction - to avoid being waylaid by strongholds that take our thoughts and mind away from the direction of God. I bought a book at my retreat, by a woman named Beth Moore [*Praying God's Word: Breaking Free from Spiritual Strongholds*, by Beth Moore; B&H Books; September 1, 2009], concerning praying God's Word. It deals with defeating strongholds (these are things in the world that take our thoughts/our minds away from God). They are forms of idolatry (which too many uninformed people think merely means worship of other "gods" and don't understand what another "god" can be - basically anything we make more important in our life than God).

I like these 2 quotes. Thanks.

Love and peace and prayers, Sally

—ɯ—

Scott (Sunday, November 29, 2009 11:44 PM)

Today (Nov 29th) is the Eighth Anniversary of the passing of George Harrison, a great man, but even more importantly a great spirit, whose message lives with us forever. As Vivekananda's writings were one of the sources of George's lifelong growing knowledge of God, Swami V and his master [Ramakrishna] step aside today, and let George deliver today's message (of awareness). [Lyrics to "Be Here Now" were included in correspondence; deleted in edited text. Interested seekers can easily find them on line.]

Hare Krishna!
OM!

Sally (Monday, November 30, 2009 9:25 PM)

Wow - I didn't realize it's been 8 years. These are good words - we need to slow down, be aware of today, now, don't be stressed about tomorrow. This is one area in which Kel has the right concept and I still struggle when it comes to my work day. I work right up to 4:15, the end of my official work day [which begins very early] and quite often I'm still working at 4:30 and if at home, even later [works at home most days; some days at office in Colorado Springs ~ 1 ½ hrs away]; then I start to shut down for the day, clean up and get ready to go and am still thinking about what I didn't get done, what I have to do tomorrow… worry…worry…worry – stress…stress…stress! Kel was ready to go at the end of the day and pick up where he left off the next day. It will always be there, and if you don't get it done today - deal with it tomorrow (they sure aren't going to fire me for not getting everything done by the end of the day!). So, he really never experienced the stress/anxiety on the job that I do or that I have (I am working to reduce that and have gotten better).

Read Philippians 4:6-7. Heard that one on the radio this morning - about not being anxious. I get very stressed/anxious this time of year and have a hard time with the concept of "be here now". I wish I didn't have to work in December. I want to be decorating for Christmas, baking, shopping/wrapping, etc and stress myself out that I won't "get it all done" although I'm not sure what would happen if I didn't get it all done. The list of what "needs" to be done is only in my head, nobody has given me a time schedule and nobody will care if I don't decorate to a certain level or standard (only Kel and I usually see it), and I'm sure you wouldn't mind if we showed up still needing to wrap gifts - so why do I let myself get that way? Do those things really matter? And will anyone remember or care later? Thanks for sharing this - it will be another reminder for me during this time of year.

Love and peace and prayers - Sally

[*Do not be anxious about anything, but in everything, by prayer and petition, with thanksgiving, present your requests to God. And the peace of God, which transcends all understanding, will guard your hearts and your minds in Christ Jesus.* **Philippians 4:6-7**; New International Version.]

—∞—

Scott (Wednesday, December 9, 2009 11:25 PM)

Subject: "and now the screaming starts…"

That is the name of an old Peter Cushing movie I believe. ["Screaming" reflected the mood I had apparently been in when composing the poem discussed in this email, *Pessimism*, included in the current volume].

You all (all y'all) know I try to keep my chin up...that part still works... and I am trying to make a journey I may have not started on without my diagnosis, but that journey is sometimes hindered by the horror of it, etc. I noted a passage in Colin Wilson's *Mind Parasites* (currently enjoying) [See Book List] that alluded to the fact that true poetry can't be reached/motivated without the sort of shock (like awareness of mental parasites dwelling in our deepest layers of mind and holding man "back") that allows entry into a level of mind we don't normally try to reach. I would never confuse myself with a poet (I'm actually just taking a break from reading Walt Whitman's "When Lilacs Last in Dooryard Bloom'd"...kind of long....), but I'm told to go ahead and get the dark out if I feel it. After everyone went to bed the other night on our RV trip, I just scribbled this out on some scrap paper [with this email, was sending electronic version for Sally to review].

I noticed as I was reading a book of translated Osip Mandelstam poems that most of his poems are just numbered; he only named a few, and despite dying at 47 (ouch....), he wrote upwards of 300-400. That being, of course, despite the hindrances of the pesky little things like arrest and exile to Urals and then Siberia during the enlightened Stalin years. He didn't have a "day job" per se...like all that medicine/science stuff. So, I'll try to finish a book or two, and a few more scientific manuscripts, but if I make it to 50 or 100 poems, would be (in addition to waste of paper or hard drive space)....a bit of a miracle; but with that denominator especially, my goal includes to be the "poet" with the highest percentage of frank usage of the word "shit" in his works.....

Despite the gloom, I actually think this poem has structural, meter, and imagery merit...and hopefully represents near the deepest I'll fall...

...whatever...ss

Sally (Thursday, December 10, 2009 8:25 PM)

50-100 poems would be quite an accomplishment, especially on top of 1-2 books AND the science/medical stuff! And highest percentage of usage of "shit" would probably be followed by usage of "amongst" - although not as often as William Boyd. [A favorite author of Scott's, two novels of whose were included in Sally's fifty birthday presents.] I also want a copy of the December 7 poem (Pearl Harbor vs Big Bend). [*Pearl Harbor Day in Big Bend National Park*, included in this collection]

—w—

Scott (Sunday, December 13, 2009 1:12 AM)

It was surprisingly good to see so many friends and loved ones at dinner tonight [Holiday party for Scott's Lab]...despite the surrealistic feeling of having a hard time walking in a very crowded restaurant filled with so many of the healthy masses.

Even though everyone there is actively working and I am not, I did not experience the strong sense of loss or absence that work related topics and colleagues had instilled in the early days post diagnosis. I enjoyed talking to Tanner (the second pathologist who joined Dallas lab, whom we knew at Vanderbilt in Nashville)-including about my novel, his kids, etc. I met a few new people, and was hugged and told "I love you" and such by a lot of people that I used to just be in the trenches with...

It was weird to be out with such fragile legs...the difficulty walking, the cane at the table, my bladder insulting tight pants (in part because the atrophy of my leg muscles, with their reduced calorie needs, is causing my belly to accumulate adipose), etc were caressed away by recognition that people who care about you, people we let in our lives and share our selves with....are now (at least tonight), not just a reminder of everything I worked so hard for and am losing. Instead, it was a reminder of the things that make us care about each other and how that love is important and "useful" at this stage of my "evolution".

And, so, as not uncommon these days, I felt compelled to scribble some poem about it; acknowledging encounters that can be strengthening and reaffirming. A poem draft is attached [*Perspective*, included in this collection]; messed with another structural thing in this one.....subtle that may be noticeable without pointing out, but the starting letters of each line make a parallel vertical story, as in IBBS (I be BS); THERE, THERE, ISGOD

Better not quit the day job just yet....

It's also time to quit procrastinating (not a luxury I have) and wrap up the book [novel started in 2004 and completed subsequent to diagnosis] and get it out.....to move on to next things

peace, ss

Sally (Sunday, December 13, 2009 9:41 PM)

Don't care what you say - I think this IS your day job now. The poem is awesome! I see and feel your evolution in this poem and in the progress from 1st poem to this poem. Also see progress and evolution in you from the dinner at the fondue restaurant for Heidi & Devette's birthday (end of evening) [closer to diagnosis and following which Scott physically displayed some outrage about his disease afterwards] to this dinner you just described. I thought about you last night and was so hoping that you had a good evening and didn't get too maudlin but that you were able to enjoy being out and being around people that know you, respect you, appreciate you and love you. Remember and hold on to that always - no matter what or how bad or how fast things happen. You have a lot of people who love you and care about you and who will care for you.

Truly this poem speaks volumes. I know you want to move forward on the novel and we will, but I really think getting your poems published could be helpful to other people going through all sorts of similar health and other issues - to see that they aren't alone in what they feel, what they experience. Your poetry could be a sort of "support group" for them. Please don't stop the flow of your thoughts and feelings - keep capturing them on paper in your late night scribbling (could be a title), and maybe later on a tape recorder.

Re your "being fat", go ahead and do the girl thing and buy some "fat" pants for times when you go out.

Love and peace and prayers and hugs, your sister

—⟋⟍—

Scott (Thursday, December 31, 2009 2:29 AM)

On knowledge and ignorance:

"But fortunately we MUST inquire into the beyond. This present, this expressed, is only one part of that unexpressed. The sense universe is, as it were, only one portion, one bit of that infinite spiritual universe projected into the plane of sense consciousness."
-Swami Vivekananda

(thought I'd keep it towards the metaphysical side tonight)

peace, ss

Sally (Thursday, December 31, 2009 10:41 AM)

Thanks for getting back to the Vivekananda messages. We need our daily spiritual readings; helps keep us focused especially as we go into the New Year. And it's nice to know there is more than just this [physical world] that we experience - and with a little effort there is something more meaningful to explore, to learn about, to attempt to know.

Keep 'em coming.

Peace and prayers and love, Sally

Excerpts from Correspondences to Family and Friends

January 2, 2010

Dear friends and relatives,

Many of you have contacted me out of love, concern, and sympathy, and I have not been very good about responding. It is difficult for me to continually or frequently put myself back in the state or condition to be able to talk about my disease and my consequent mood as often as such personal correspondence would mandate.

As many of you know, I was diagnosed with ALS (Lou Gehrig's disease) in April 2009. I don't want to get into a lot of specifics about my disease and course. In brief, I presented primarily with left hip flexor weakness, left quad (thigh) atrophy, a possible left foot drop, and some possible milder, similar weakness in my right leg. As expected, all of these symptoms/signs have progressed. For example, I can no longer lift my left foot and this means common tripping, improved by my first official artificial devise: a left foot brace (that needs some artistic decorations I believe). I can no longer walk up stairs without some support like a banister and using both arms/hands. 2010 will hence likely see greater use of a cane and eventual wheelchair. If there is a good side to my specific condition (besides forcing a workaholic physician-scientist to focus on spiritual/personal things), I have some "favorable" prognostic features. ALS apparently has a proven predilection for smart/nice people. I'm trying to destroy most or all of my "ego" from a spiritual perspective, but hopefully they at least won't do tests to find me an exception, and decide that I'm not very nice.....

I have not approached my disease with the objective rigor of my usual or past scientific self (e.g., by reading/studying, as I have done, say, for my prostate cancer research). To me, this would not serve any benefit compared to what I have been doing with my time. I am taking the only FDA approved drug for ALS. I have focused on spiritual issues (some of which were too long ignored) and family time (also too long ignored). And, as might be expected by those who know me, I have been doing a lot of reading, which my past schedule also did not allow as much of as I may have liked. As per some requests, I may post my list of read books, as they have been beneficial to me, and they are selected books that are very worth while to read.

Family time has included a few (three to date) RV trips. It has been fun to watch Heidi and Kel master the driving and other operations of the 39 or 40 foot A-class "rigs" we take out.

Thanks for all your thoughts and prayers. It has been a bizarre and intense, mentally, physically, and emotionally challenging year, and the physical journey downward and spiritual journey hopefully upward are still sort of just beginning for me. I hope that many or all of you will not wait till peri-death to explore the latter. Do not feel sorry for me. As George Harrison so well reminded us, the minute you are born you begin to die. If you believe in the immortal spirit, 78 or 48 or 8 divided by infinity is essentially still zero. This physical life is so transient. I hope it doesn't take a terminal diagnosis for all of us to realize that.

I welcome your prayers!

Love and Peace,
ss

"I notice that when my mind is united with God the suffering of the body is left aside"
-The Divine Sri Ramakrishna

OM

—⟋⟋⟍—

April 20, 2010

Quick (for me to squirt out…maybe not to read…) update on my physical status and the often surrealistic adjustments that Heidi does such a great job in facilitating:

- In addition to various ramps, the biggest alteration is modification of our front meditation room to put in an actual elevator…yes, an elevator. On my past long list of eventual acquisitions, this never cracked the top 1000. However, the good news is that it supposedly adds ~10 % value to a house. They did a great job, so it looks like it was there when the house was built. Automatic outer and inner doors, and it goes right up to our previously very (and now still moderately) oversized master closet, so it allows me to have easier access to our more Scott-friendly master bath…for all those bodily function things… (By the way, if anyone wants to do the "Love in the Elevator" thing, bring your own partner, as masturbation doesn't count, and help in this regard is beyond the scope of our host duties.)

-Walking is essentially non-existent (left leg largely decorative, and not particularly in an attractive way unless you have a fetish for quad atrophy and swollen feet…and right leg following behind on same but delayed course), except for short distances with cane and longer distances with the rollator/ walker (still gives me a bit of a "grandma" feel, but it has a basket you can store a shit load of books and other things in, carry beers from garage fridge to patio with, etc.). [Compatible with expected progression, loss of any ability to walk

139

has ensued in the time between this correspondence and book editing, with full time dependence on power chair]

- The Made in Switzerland (by the company that makes Rolls Royce's seem practically priced) power chair is here. This will give me time to adjust to its controls prior to necessity...and herein comes the "sad" part:

-We're getting a Mini-Van!...a modified one that can accommodate the chair, and of course has all the bells and whistles, so i can like watch DVDs while i recline in my chair in mid seat, but...in addition to the "shock" of the mini-van thing (after all, we currently have three vehicles if you include the ol' jeep, none with even true back seats...), as it is new and majorly modified and we got our CLK 500 and Boxter S convertibles with a couple thousand miles on them already, the van cost more than the Mercedes and the Porsche...how's that for irony...

- Final draft of first novel done and in the hands of a couple chosen readers for (hopefully) minor editing suggestions

- I'll update the reading list, but from the spiritual side in the meantime, as I've been in a Robert Bly mood lately, and since the concept of "neurons" has particular application to someone facing the "challenge" (the politically correct term) of ALS, here's a poem in case there's anyone out there besides me that gives a shit about great poetry. [Correspondence included the hauntingly lovely poem, "The Neurons Who Watch Birds", by Robert Bly. Deleted in edited text.]

Peace (and keep an eye out for me...in the stars...or the ring in your bath tub...and if the latter, be gentle when scrubbing me away and rinsing me down the drain)

ss

April 21, 2010: One Year Anniversary of My Diagnosis of ALS

I can still see this scene in my hopefully growing mind:

Dr. T (sitting down to discuss the EMG results): "It's not good. Everywhere I stick, I'm getting a neuropathic pattern."

Scott (displaying medical knowledge he maybe regrets having): "ALS?" (But it wasn't really a question, was it)

Dr. T: "I'm afraid so"

I glanced over at Heidi. Tears were welling up in her eyes…the beautiful big brown eyes I'd been staring into for sixteen years and yet in some way, as if seeing them changed…something new…and then they started to flow down her lovely cheeks. She reached a hand up to ineffectively wipe some away.

Scott: "How long?"

Dr. T: "Two to five years. Depending on how fast you progress. Let's see…you started feeling weakness in January… (no further interpretation, no expression as to whether good or bad).

After a pause: "I advise all patients diagnosed with ALS to get a second opinion."

Enter stage left: Objectivity. We discuss practical aspects of whom to see, and (as we already know what the answer is going to be), where we may want follow-up (location of clinics, etc.)

Dr. T: "I'll let you two stay in here for a while…to gather yourselves."

One year later (a year of saying a steady goodbye to certain bodily functions and hello to various forms of insanity, not always welcome): No room is big enough, and no time is probably long enough. We've been trying to gather "ourselves" ever since.

(ss 4/20/2010….4/21 may just be a little too painful to think about these often sad Earthly things)

The Bucket List: Books Read and Learned From Since ALS Diagnosis

When I was first diagnosed with ALS, a few friends/relatives politely inquired regarding my possible "bucket list". I have had a good life, filled with opportunities. Much of it was spent learning. Increasingly over the last many years, I have had resources that could have allowed for various adventures. I have pursued some, but not as many as I could have if that were "my thing". My family traveled a lot when I was growing up, and my wife and I traveled a fair amount in the first ten years of our marriage, with highlights including Hawaii, New York, Italy, and especially Africa (South Africa, Botswana, Zambia) in 2008. Recently, prior to my diagnosis and when money and maybe even time were more available, though, growing anxiety and commitment to a new laboratory business may have kept me from going away as often as I probably should have. However, daily enjoyments have always included hanging out with Heidi, with shared passion for good food, wine, football, and music.

I have always passionately given myself to learning and attempting to understand everything I've been exposed to. To me, the most interesting journeys are on the inside. Since I didn't sleep very much until I took time off after the ALS diagnosis, my friends and family have speculated (e.g., if you do the math) that I've had as many waking hours as most may have during an expected normal length lifetime. When facing the harsh reality that I would likely prematurely run out of time, I intuited that I needed to work on my spiritual life. Hence, if I were going to finally take time away from my usual (past) life pursuits, it wouldn't necessarily be for sky diving or visiting the Seven Wonders of the World. In addition to raiding the wine cellar and spending time with family, reading, learning, trying to understand, and seeing truly are more in keeping with my nature and my spiritual goals.

Peter Noll, an intelligent lawyer with advanced cancer and likely less than one year to live at the time he authored *In the Face of Death*, noted that when death is looming one reads more, with emphasis on more important things. I have found this to be true for me. The list of books that I have encountered in my particular journey may seem somewhat heterogeneous and not obviously connected. This may be a consequence, in part, of a perpetually broad range of interests, as in my professional science career.

However, reading and other intellectual exercises are only adjuncts in a spiritual journey. They can support the quest, perhaps in part by removing certain hindrances. Hence, the books I have read and continue to read have been the kind that I thought could be helpful as well as enjoyable. In many cases, reading one book has led to others, in a growing branching and interconnected network of hopefully synergistically enlightening encounters. The books have included those of a spiritual nature, classic or highly regarded novels, collections of poetry, and psychology and physical science books (particularly with philosophical or religious implications). I think these books have been useful to facilitate an increase of spiritual awareness, to help the asking of large questions, to provide inner strength to address the possible answers to those questions, and to deal with implications to those answers. In particular, they continue to help "kill the filter", to remove some preconceptions originating in scientific reductionism or other prejudices and to enable a more open minded approach to consciousness and spirituality.

In what follows, such books are listed, with comments and reviews offered in the context of the above perspective. I have often tried to indicate why I read them, as well as how they helped me. Perhaps this may encourage other ALS or otherwise terminal patients (and their supporters) to read these or related books. Further, it is the author's hope that this could also initiate a dialogue (e.g., as web-based posts) that will allow others to comment on these or to suggest other books that they believe may be helpful to patients and their families undergoing similar challenges and journeys.

Much of the spiritual reading has involved certain aspects of Hinduism or Vedantic philosophy. As I became more exposed to such ideas, I came to realize that the beautiful spiritual messages matched best my past (and long ignored) beliefs, including those that sat comfortably in the setting of true objective scientific knowledge, as well as the crucial elements for true growth in a newly awakened spirituality. Some of my reading and parallel thinking has ushered in a necessary reassessment of the ability of science to address all the questions of our existence and consciousness. I still believe that there are fundamental laws of nature. However, the meaning of these has changed somewhat for me, perhaps in an expansion of reawakened prior beliefs. I readily acknowledge that not only is science incomplete, but there are certain things that are (essentially by definition) outside the realm of science (i.e., the kinds of things that can't be proven or disproven by the scientific method, now or perhaps ever; those sorts of things commonly regarded as metaphysical). However, as a true scientist (which means adherence to scientific methods, but with an open mind) I naturally found myself always turned off by closed-minded, unsubstantiated yet rigid claims to knowledge regarding those "big questions" (even if not amenable to conventional scientific investigation). This is not an uncommon philosophy among scientists. However, a subset of scientists have become equally dogmatic, holding to the reductionist approach to understanding existence, the universe, and all things within it despite the absurdity of some of the notions necessary to maintain this stance. Such individuals may reach the point of ignoring or trying to destroy even objective demonstration of things outside their theories and realms of investigation, such that they are as closed minded as the most fanatical brain-washed religious zealots.

I have thus found myself particularly drawn to and strengthened by the teachings of Sri Ramakrishna and Swami Vivekananda. In contrast to the common closed mindedness of many religious leaders, with rigorous exclusion of the ideas of others, these great souls recognized that all paths lead to God. Further, I (and many of my scientific colleagues) believe that the laws of science (or nature) that we as mankind have "deduced" or "discovered" so far are fundamentally related to the existence that the Creator put in place. Understanding things, as in being able to express a cosmological event mathematically or relating a disease to a specific mutation in a gene sequence does NOT *a priori* exclude a creative force and a divine principle. In fact, to me, it supports it. We are either one with or a part of God, depending on your philosophy. So, biological and social evolution towards divine wisdom seems like a logical progression in a cosmos in which an incomprehensible supreme soul or consciousness manifests in a physical universe according to the "laws" put in place. Thus, I also particularly appreciate the idea emphasized by Swami Vivekananda that nothing expressed within a spiritual philosophy should contradict observations and conclusions of well-done science.

However, as also stressed by such great spiritual teachers, God or the Self cannot be reached or realized by intellectual means. One must feel and directly experience the Divine, not generate God like a solid powder following some key chemical processes in a lab experiment. Hence, broadening my realm of thinking and feeling has been essential in my spiritual journey. Perhaps as a consequence, I have become strongly attracted to poetry. Great poetry can expand one's mind and thinking more effectively than sticks of dynamite placed between the cerebral hemispheres. And, it can reach directly to some place different.

I had not read poetry in essentially 28 years. Revisiting poetry may have initially been part of grasping at anything to ease the horror of the physical decline and emotional pain of what I was going through. More than ever anticipated, poetry has become soul expanding at a crucial time in my own little life and its ongoing transitions, by showing me that there are no limits to how one thinks, how one feels, and how one inquires about himself or herself. Poetry, as with other real art, is the boundless form of expression of all mankind's greatest and often unrecognized strengths and our most tragic weaknesses. It is a vehicle for the expression of thoughts way outside the realm of science, those within my ever expanding and maybe unreachable infinite target-zone. As I read the masterful words of Blake, Yeats, Wordsworth, Rilke, Neruda, Mandelstam, Akhmatova, Apollinaire, Baudelaire, Dickinson, Whitman, Bly, Pinsky, Roethke, and Wright, I know that all the spirits of all things suffering AND celebrating are connected.

Each book read seems to awaken a desire to read several others. This has actually evolved into a therapeutic strategy. We have stated (likely beyond our power and authority) that God can't take me until I've finished everything on my reading list. Hence, one can easily see how clever the survival tactic is of continually adding more and more books to the huge "to read" stack.

The collective authorship that humanity has engaged upon is, in some ways, a micro-model of the "oneness" of all things within our species and the entire cosmos...of everything. I have been lucky and blessed to stumble into the universe at this time and place.

Peace to all searchers everywhere
ss

Om!
Peace.Peace.Peace.

I-Me-Mine, by George Harrison. Peace to this great soul! When my Neurologist confirmed my ALS diagnosis, the first of his particularly useful comments that have since continued was, "Spiritual people do better." Although I wasn't sure if he was simply presenting an objective medical fact or providing a more specific helpful hint based on what he'd discerned about me thus far, I told him when leaving that I would go home and listen to my George Harrison tapes. This was ridiculous, of course, and probably a consequence of my ongoing shock, as after all, they're CDs. However, a place with at least some familiarity and comfort for a music fan seemed a reasonable starting point. This book was originally published in 1980 as a leather-bound limited release and made readily available in 2002 in paperback form, with a new introduction by Olivia Harrison, after George's death in 2001. So, as I initially fell away from work that I'd prepared my whole life for, I started with the words of one of my musical and spiritual heroes. The relatively brief autobiographical text came from George's narrative to long-time friend Derek Taylor, who also inserted notes. The wisdom and love conveyed with such sincerity by a man who was humble despite being one of the most famous human beings on the planet demonstrate the strength of George's spirituality. As anyone familiar with The Beatles knows, his search began early in his life and busy career. The included pictures reveal the growing light inside a gentle sage progressing through the material world. The lyrics for the songs written by George during the Beatles and his solo career up to that point are included, with brief comments related to their inspiration, as well as enjoyable reproductions of original hand written forms. The simple beauty of the lyrics, especially of the songs of spiritual striving and realizing, continue to be uplifting to me. And listening to these songs presented with George's sweet voice, perfectly integrated diverse guitar skills, and masterful attention to production on the various CDs (including from some "albums" I'd not had before) is a recurring gift. Learning about George's own spiritual journey (including as detailed more in Joshua Greene's biography) also helped steer me more towards Eastern ideas, including to teachings of Srila Prabhupāda.

The Tao of Physics, by Fritjof Capra. As a prior Physics major, I had this book from the beginning of medical and graduate school (as evidenced by the scribble on the cover by the infant Travis, my son), but I had not read it until recently. While reviewing some of the major observations and principles of modern quantum physics, the book draws attention to the similarities of the philosophical implications and the crucial concepts of oneness in Eastern religions (such as Buddhism, Taoism, Zen, and Hinduism). As a scientist, this well written modern classic made me more receptive to the nature of the ideas of spiritual awareness that great Eastern Mystics have had forever. I became particularly more attracted to Hinduism.

Bhagavad Gita, translated by Swami Prabhavananda/Christopher Isherwood. Heidi had a copy already, and now it was time for me to read it. The *Gita* is actually contained within the epic Sanskrit poem, *The Mahabharata*. Typically printed by itself, the *Gita* is perhaps the most popular religious text in Hinduism. Set in the background of an impending battle between the Pandava brothers (sons of Kunti, related to the God Krishna) and the Kauravas, their jealous cousins, the *Gita* is divided into eighteen sections. It is presented as a dialogue between Arjuna, a great archer, and Krishna, incarnated in human form and serving as his charioteer. Arjuna is hesitant to fight his cousins, but as Krishna teaches him: a person is bound by his dharma (one's duty within divine law) to engage in the world, while at the same time remaining unattached to it; and that if his cause is just, then he is doing his duty, rather than fighting for gain or glory. Such is the path of Karma-Yoga. The *Gita* also contains sacred words from Krishna about the nature of Brahman, the Absolute (related to Vedanta philosophy and Jnana-Yoga), as well as belief in a personal God (Bhakti-Yoga). Different paths to God is an important aspect of Hinduism. The theme of accepting and dealing with one's fate was particularly relevant in a struggle to accept my disease and prognosis.

The Upanishads, translated by Swami Paramananda. Heidi already had a copy of this particular translation, which includes the Isa-, Katha-, and Kena-Upanishads. I read it twice, and have since obtained the four volume version of eleven major Upanishads, translated by Swami Nikhilananda. The *Upanishads* are sacred literature that convey the basis of the Vedanta school of Hindu philosophy (see Glossary). There are 108 Upanishads, with several of the major Upanishads represented in commonly available translations. They are composed partly in verse, partly in prose, and commonly take the form of dialogue between student and teacher. Deviating from the practice of rituals as emphasized in earlier portions of the Vedas, the Upanishads deal with the ultimate truths, such as the nature of the cosmos and the identity of Self and God. I believe that we, as our souls, are all either identical with God (as regarded within the non-dualist philosophy contained in the *Upanishads*) or are parts of God, as the Divine Consciousness. The

Upanishads are sparse, glorious, and beautiful reflections on the essence of our divine souls and the oneness of all things.

How to Understand Hinduism, by Jean-Christophe Demariaux. I picked this book up in passing to provide a bit more background to my readings. In addition to the useful background on the history of Hinduism and the confusing array of the many deities, the chapter on Modern Reformers helped expose me to the ideas of Sri Ramakrishna, encouraging further readings which have lit a flame inside.

The Unbearable Lightness of Being, by Milan Kundera; translated by Michael Henry Heim. Thanks for the recommendation by Katy Rigler. This fantastic novel is a somewhat haunting portrayal of the lives of individuals, geographically dispersed over time, but primarily occurring under the oppressive regime of Communism in Czechoslovakia, following the Russian invasion in 1968. In this context, universal issues of humanity and relationships are explored, with philosophical musings by Kundera interlaced with the story of his characters. Underneath the somewhat tragic dictum of "ein mal ist keinmal" ("one time is equal to no time"), the young Czech physician Tomas immerses himself in casual sexual liaisons as a subconscious surrogate for any sense of control that would evade him in the frustrating and nonsensical circumstances imposed by the ruling forces. His partner Tereza, whose feelings are opened particularly in powerful dreams, must live within the torment of deciding whether to put up with his infidelity. Other interesting characters fill out the narrative as the story unfolds to explore a plethora of possible themes. The decisions we make in what seems a haphazard or coincidental manner have major bearing and determining effects on individual lives. I particularly liked the expressed notion of judgment of a society based on its treatment of its animals. Further, any book that includes an analysis in the philosophy of excrement and the potential implications of a God possessing intestines was right up my alley at a time of questioning all light vs. heavy aspects of life. My son Travis (a fan of Kundera) subsequently bought me *Immortality* (the book...) for Christmas 2009.

The Bible – yes, my dear friends and relatives, I'm reading The Bible, including: select scriptures, thanks to Sally; The Gospel of John; Romans; The Gospel of Luke; Acts; Job (thought this would be tough after the ALS diagnosis, so took a while to get to); The Gospel of Matthew.

The Gospel of Sri Ramakrishna – Abridged edition; translated from original Bengali and with Introduction by Swami Nikhilananda. This is likely the most important book I've ever read. (See also Spiritual Correspondences Section above). This book is composed of accounts of daily interactions and sayings recorded by a householder devotee ("M") who came to Ramakrishna after the Master had been worshipping and teaching for many years. The book is in dialogue form (like classic Socratic/Platonic method), and each day's session can be read quickly-as a sort of daily devotional, and perhaps meditated upon. The setting is thus toward the end of Ramakrishna's subsequently shortened life, including as he was suffering and preparing to die from throat cancer. These circumstances further indicated the strength and truth in his beautiful and simple, yet powerful, teachings. No more direct and humble words and parables about seeing and knowing God could likely be found anywhere.

Memories, Dreams, Reflections, by C.G. Jung (recorded/edited by Aniela Jaffe; translated by Richard and Clara Winston). Thanks again to Katy Rigler for the recommendation. This essentially autobiographical compilation of thoughts toward the end of Jung's life is a bit of a tough read, but is SO worth it. For those unfamiliar with Jung, like I was at the time, this book can also serve as a bit of a detailed introduction to much of his life-long thoughts, although it is not intended as a summary of prior works. There is a fine line between intrigued by and addicted to Jung. His refreshingly original insight into psychological, religious, and social ideas is a good companion to have during a period of deep reflection, including on the Self. As with a slate-wiping near death experience or a conversation with a really wise alien at a bar, his thoughts have infused my approach to other literature, some of my poetry, and even my spiritual contemplations.

A Short Life of Swami Vivekananda by Swami Tejasananda; Advaita Ashrama. This is a brief biography that served to inform my subsequent readings of Vivekananda, including what happened after Ramakrishna's death, details on his monumental trips to the West, and his meditative studies when returning to India.

Vivekananda World Teacher. His Teachings on the Spiritual Unity of Humankind, edited by Swami Adiswarananda (past director of the Ramakrishna-Vivekananda Center in N.Y.), with an outstanding Introductory Essay by Swami Nikhilananda (founder of the Center). This book is a collection from various sources, primarily lectures that Swami Vivekananda gave in the West, following his rise to popularity at the First Parliament of Religions in Chicago in 1899. These are very conversationally phrased presentations on such topics as the equality of religions, desire for a universal religion, and philosophical considerations of various avatars, such as Buddha, Christ, and Krishna. Included are some correspondences, poems, and opinions expressed by others on the man and his message. Vivekananda's philosophy toward religion was highly enlightened and conducive to a true humanity. No wonder his visits to the West and his message were so well received by those capable of clear and independent thinking.

The Atheist and the Holy City. Encounters and Reflections, by Geoge Klein; translated by Theodore and Ingrid Friedmann. This was another book I bought about twenty years ago, as the combination of science and philosophy made it appealing. Yet, I never got around to reading it. In general, the demands of medical and research education and training and the types of sports- and bar-associated activities engaged to counter them did not allow for much leisure reading for many years. A beneficiary of belonging to a pack-rat, it survived at least five moves and when I looked at it again following April 2009, the conditions were right and I read it on one of our RV trips. Klein had been an internationally recognized scientist for many decades, including as the head of the Tumor Biology Department at Karolinska Institute in Sweden (and serving on the Nobel Prize Committee). Author of maybe 800-1000 scientific papers, he had not previously written "non-science" literature before. This collection of essays grew out of a forward he was asked to write for Peter Noll's book, *In the Face of Death*. Klein is an atheist and a hard core scientist, but a wonderful humanist. He was one of the 200,000 rescued Jews in Budapest who were about to be exterminated by the Nazis, and lost all his family in the Holocaust. Masterfully handled topics relate modern science to issues of the interactions of human beings, explored in the complex inter-lacings of psychology, poetry, and tragedy at the level of individuals and society. For example, in "Ultima Thule", Klein talks with German geneticist Benno-Muller Hill in a provocative consideration of the role of scientists in the emergence of Germany's pre-WW II suspect approach to genetics and race classification and later, in the actual execution of the Holocaust. Moral battlegrounds included experimental use by physician scientists of procured and banked tissues of concentration camp victims. Approaching this book as a scientist, it was an opportunity to expand the scope or even alter orientation of thinking related to some issues that have faced or are facing mankind. This book won the Swedish equivalent of the Pulitzer Prize and is readily approachable by the non-scientist reader as well.

The Beginner's Guide to Jungian Psychology, by Robin Robertson. After feeling like I'd been exposed to an important avenue of piercing thought, free of conventional religious and social constraints, in *Memories, Dreams, Reflections*, I wanted to learn more about Jung's psychology. This is a well written, easy to read introduction to some of the major concepts, such as personality types, the Shadow, the Animus, and the Self. At the risk of being disowned by some former colleagues perhaps, I have reflected upon the primary function and secondary functions of what I perceive as may be my own personality type. This has maybe facilitated a growing awareness of what further developments I should be more receptive to, including from unconscious sources, such as dreams. Other ALS patients are likely very familiar with themes of some of the common bad dreams and nightmares ushered in by the diagnosis (e.g., physical impairments even beyond those already actually present preventing escapes or even normal function and such). Yet, even in these and increasingly within others dreams, I begin to recognize aspects of possible development regarding fears and projections in Shadow figures and needs from Animus symbols that will hopefully progress to compliment other conscious efforts in Self-realization.

Briefing for a Descent into Hell, by Doris Lessing. I had only read her novel *The Fifth Child* before, but had this book for some time. She calls it "Inner Space Fiction", and in parallel to reading this unique novel, I have gotten a bit intrigued by some of the psychology from the same period of the late 60's (e.g., see R.D. Laing below). Many were realizing how screwed up the world we were making was…and it has only gotten worse, of course. In this disturbing yet provocative novel of social commentary, the delusions of a newly psychotic man relate to a perceived reawakening of a cosmic mission to check the human destructive tendencies toward self and nature. Regarded by some as a tough read; but well worth it, especially for any of those who believe or are at least willing to entertain the belief that insanity may not be that crazy and could even be a proper response to the modern world and/or a way of connecting to the ignored wisdom of Nature. Readers should not get bogged down on the first third or so, which is told as the delusions of the lead character. This portion is rather lyrical and interesting, but even casual (quicker) reading of this part will impart enough appreciation to support understanding the rest of the book.

Pieta, by George Klein; translated by Theodore and Ingrid Friedmann. After reading *The Atheist and the Holy* City, I was eager to read Klein's subsequent book. In the context of horrific events from Hiroshima, Auschwitz, suicides, and speculation on where society's response to the AIDS epidemic may progress (from perspective of late 1980s), Klein further explores aspects of individual and collective humanity in essays that were particularly good and serious company for my state of mind. As with his prior book, any aspects of included science that have become dated over the past two decades do not detract at all from the force of the insightful messages. In addition to the intelligent and provocative writing in *Pieta*, if not for Klein (a broadly diversified scholar), I would not have specifically sought out more of the lovely sad poetry of Hungarian Attila József, maybe not pursued the utterly transforming poems of Bohemian/German Rilke, and even confronted specific writings by Camus as well (as there is much poetry and literature reference and analysis in Klein's essays).

The World We Used to Live In. Remembering the Powers of the Medicine Men, by Vine Deloria, Jr. We obtained this book at Arches National Park on one of our RV trips. It is a series of topic-organized reports and descriptions of documented acts and aspects related to the connection of Native Americans to Nature and the Spirits. Settings range from hunting, to war, to healing, to spiritual journeys. Especially to someone searching for potentially broader (even if less easily reproduced, conveniently packaged, and marketable) truths than traditionally exposed to in our culture, it is a great reminder of how certain societies of mankind used to be far better connected to Nature, to each other, their ancestors, and to the Cosmos/Spirits.

Selected Poems by Attila József, translated by Peter Hargitai. (Review refers to book, copyright 2005; iUnivese, Inc., Lincoln, NE.) Along with various anthologies of primarily English language poetry, this book is essentially where my resurrected reading of poetry began after my diagnosis. József wrote in Hungary between WWI and WWII. Regarded as schizophrenic (or otherwise mentally ill), he eventually killed himself at just age 32. His poetry is beautiful and tragic, and it may be equally valid to consider him a sensitive voice for the real insanity that existed in the society of post-War Europe/Hungary. Hargitai had won an award from the Academy of American Poets for a previous translated collection of József poems. This 2005 book contains 100 poems to commemorate the 100th anniversary of Attila József's birth in 1905. The translations in this small book masterfully capture the soft power of the deceptively simple verse, with word combinations that perhaps only such a tortured mind and heart could bring together. Some favorites include "Elegy", "Ode", "Night in the Ghetto", "Sometimes Islands", "The Man Spoke", "I'm Leaving Everything", "Hearsay", and "Weary Man". Faced with past abandonment in childhood and the widespread suffering of his fellow countrymen, this fragile poet spoke both of the sadness of his people, as in poems like "A Tree Here, a Tree There" and "Stones", as well as the sadness of the single soul. Many times lately I have felt as if: *I'm perched solidly / on nothing's branch. / The small body shivers / to receive heaven* (from "Perched on Nothing's Branch"). As ALS is teaching me and has sadly taught so many others, sometimes suffering can occur even in the best of times and places. And we brace to face our horror, as in speaking to God: *I hold my breath to die. / And if you don't beat me, / I'll swear up and down / that you have no face. / And then I'll stare you down* (last stanza from "Spring Suddenly From the Tide"). Sometimes to heal our hearts, we need verse that reaches down and opens something raw inside.

Teachings of Swami Vivekananda, from the Advaita Ashrama. This compact book is a collection of sayings from Vivekananda, organized by topic (See also Spiritual Correspondences Section). Many of these topics are broadly applicable to people of all faiths and his teachings are a wonderful extension of the ideas of Sri Ramakrishna.

If interested in any of the described teachings of Ramakrishna or Vivekananda, these and many other inexpensive books can be obtained from the Ramakrishna-Vivekananda Center (http://www.ramakrishna.org/index.htm).

Answer to Job, by C. G. Jung; in *The Portable Jung*, edited by Joseph Campbell. This work was apparently very controversial. Jung's work strikes me as an interesting fusion of empirical science and spirituality, accompanied by innovative thought processes and insight that hovers between intuition and imagination. *Answer to Job* is nothing if not bold and staggeringly interesting. It addresses particular issues regarding man's concept of God, the necessity for The Book of Revelation as a consequence of the post-Christ ideas/attitudes of the Christian Church, concepts of Evil, the tragedy and cost of the loss of Sophia and Wisdom in Christianity, and the benefit of the eventual Assumption of Mary in The Catholic Church. I hope to read much more of Jung as time and mental energy allows, and have begun penetrating several volumes of *The Collected Works*.

Morphic Resonance. The Nature of Formative Causation, by Rupert Sheldrake. This is a 2009 updated version of the original *New Science of Life* published in 1981. I was initially interested in reading this book in pursuit of some theories underlying the possible inheritance of acquired characteristics, in part as research for a future novel, currently in a precarious embryonic stage. However, I was also interested to see some suggestions for factors affecting properties and behaviors of systems and organisms besides inherent physical properties (e.g., for inanimate systems) or particularly likely not adequate, mechanistically cherished primary genetic information (i.e., in living systems). When Sheldrake originally published his theories (presented in this updated book) in the early 1980s (near the start of the "Molecular Biology Revolution"), he was regarded by many as a heretic. Sheldrake postulates that morphogenetic fields (as external factors) can act on morphic germs within systems and organisms (optimized for these fields) so as to impart familiar observed properties through so-called morphic resonance. Morphogenic fields could account for a wide array of how things are in our world, such as crystal structure in chemical systems, the form and movement of plants, morphogenesis in embryos, all the way to movements and behavior in animals and humans. Past forms and behaviors influence present organisms through direct, but likely immaterial, connections across time and space. Since nothing is known along the lines of what would be analogous to physical properties or "mechanisms" of action of such fields, much of the book is descriptive and speculative. However, there is emerging quality-experiment derived data consistent with these theories (some elaborated in the book), and Sheldrake presents other well thought out experiments for future support. One can apparently even participate in some experiments through Internet-based mechanisms via Sheldrake's website. Emerging data from more conventional biomedical research channels indicates some potential epigenetic mechanisms (i.e., those involving alterations other than changes in the underlying DNA sequence, such as chemical modification of DNA bases or changes in DNA-associated proteins) for inheritance of acquired traits in thus far limited contexts. "Baby steps" to open-mindedness towards things potentially falling within the realm of old-guard condescended psychic or paranormal or otherwise hog-wash phenomena may allow for increased funding for even more elaborate and sophisticated legitimate and objective research targeting even more powerful results.

Sometimes, as science gets a bit constipated, conventional, and conservative, with progress seeming to come slow in some areas and not coming at all in some things that look like brick walls or insurmountable mountains, thinking REALLY outside the status quo box is required (say for example, in Einstein's theories of relativity and early ideas regarding light quanta.....we also know what happened there).

Darkness Visible. A Memoir of Madness, by William Styron. This is a personal account by the Pulitzer Prize winning novelist (e.g., *Sophie's Choice*) of his horrific bout with depression. For anyone who has ever suffered from primary depression or experienced a loved one with primary depression, I should think this would be a powerful and rewarding book to read. For those with ALS, depression is a familiar companion. This often grim account encourages confrontation and can emerge as uplifting.

The Politics of Experience, by R.D. Laing. This masterpiece of psychology, written in the late 1960s, addresses possible causes of schizophrenia and issues of adjustment in the context of our misguided society and its present off-track course. One of the most important and provocative books I've read, presenting ideas that I found myself receptive to during a spiritual journey in which personal, religious, and societal issues are becoming re-addressed or addressed in more depth than ever before.

Here Comes the Sun. The Spiritual and Musical Journey of George Harrison, by Joshua M. Greene. This was a birthday present from Heidi. It focuses particularly on George's relationship with young Krishna devotees (followers of Srila Prabhupāda), whom he learned from and supported, including in the production of some of their music and providing support for temples and residences. Well researched with many probing insights on topics less focused on in traditional biographies of members of the Beatles. An excellent book about a great human/spirit, and a good companion read to some of the books related to Krishna and Prabhupāda, described below.

The Selected Poetry of Ranier Maria Rilke, edited/translated by Stephen Mitchell, with an introduction by Robert Hass. This collection includes poems from the entire life span of this most gifted poet, including the *Duino Elegies* and large portions of the *Sonnets to Orpheus*. This book includes the original German (for those with far greater foreign language skills than mine) and the highly regarded English translations (for folks like me) on opposite facing pages. The introduction wonderfully puts these incredibly powerful poems in personal and psychological perspective. Rilke is probably my favorite poet now.

Selected Writings of Guillaume Apollinaire, translated and introduction by Roger Shattuck. I put emphasis upon reading the verse, especially from his poetry books *Alcools* and *Calligrammes*. This collection includes the original French and the English translations on opposite facing pages. A larger than life figure, from leading the Avant-garde scene in Paris in the early 20th century to being accused and briefly imprisoned for stealing the Mona Lisa, Apollinaire wrote beautiful poetry that celebrates life's wonders with the passion and intelligence that he apparently lived it.

The Myth of Sisyphus, by Albert Camus, in *The Myth of Sisyphus and other Essays*, translated by Justin O'Brien. (See also notes to poem *Cruel Teacher* for brief description of Sisyphus in Mythology). In a somewhat "existential" essay analyzing (and essentially negating) other past philosophies including that of Kierkegaard, Camus elevates the tragically and eternally punished Sisyphus to the status of the "absurd" hero. Camus also considers whether the "absurd" is reflected in the masterful works of Dostoevsky and, more likely, in those of Kafka. ALS and other terminal patients may not have any problem recognizing the feelings of despair when pondering man's potentially miserable status of being both finite and aware of that finitude (the essence of the dilemma reflected in the term "absurd"). Upon pondering this and other readings and closing my eyes, though, I prefer to allow a little (or a lot) more room for a somewhat more spiritual attitude towards something more inside of me than transient existence-sustaining food and water and feces. However, perhaps to keep the mind open or to hopefully more bravely face the bummer that inevitable death inevitably presents to us all, I was sufficiently impressed and empowered to subsequently read novels by both Camus and Kafka (see below).

The Mind Parasites, by Colin Wilson. I read the 2005 version of the 1967 classic, with a provocative introduction by Gary Lachman (former bass player for band Blondie and author of well-regarded books on the occult and other esoteric topics) and new afterward by Colin Wilson. This intelligent and interesting novel explores psychological issues related to the untapped potential of the human mind in the setting of a thrilling science fiction story (think psychokinetic driven space travel meets archaeology meets Freud/Jung on psychedelic drugs).

The Immoralist, by André Gide; translated by David Watson, with an Introduction by Alan Sheridan (Penguin Books). A brief, but powerful novel that is likely a good example of why this French novelist of the early 20th century won the Nobel Prize for Literature. (See notes to the poem *On Reading Gide's Immoralist*, which contains a brief plot summary).

The Journey Home. Autobiography of an American Swami, by Radhanath Swami. This book was a birthday present from Sally. It was an extraordinary read, particularly at the place I was and still am "stepping" with infantile feet. Wonderfully told tale of a physically, mentally, and spiritually large and fascinating journey of a young American making his way across the world (hitchhiking, in the early 1970s without any money, across Europe, Turkey, Afghanistan, and Pakistan) to India, and eventually to Bhakti Yoga and Krishna Devotion.

Light of the Bhagavata, by A.C. Bhaktivedanta Swami Prabhupāda (founder of ISKCON). This book was a Christmas present from Sally. Emphasizing a brief section of the sacred Hindu text *Śrīmad-Bhāgavatam*, this lovely little book (~150 pages, but with ~50 color prints, and still under ten dollars for hard bound) illustrates man's devotional purpose in the context of a celebration of the beauty found in nature. Integrating simply stated lessons on Krishna devotion with breath-taking matched illustrations in the Chinese Gongbi style by master artist Madam Li Yuen Sheng, this can be nicely read as a daily devotional book. For me, it was also a nice parallel to other readings related to Krishna consciousness.

The Selected Poems of Osip Mandelstam, translated by Clarence Brown and W.S. Merwin, with a good introduction by Brown. A moderately large collection, spanning the entire but shortened lifespan of the legendary Russian poet. Mandelstam was prevented from publishing much of his work during the early Stalin regime, and then was exiled to the Urals in 1934 and died in 1937 at the beginning of his second exile. Linked to the Alchemist school of poetry (in his early career) and initially celebrated by his country, his wife had to commit his later poetry to memory so that it would not be lost as a consequence of the oppressive regime endured in the last half of his life. The tenderly strong poetry of his exile years reflects his fragile state as a consequence of his past torture and the harsh living conditions. His words came from a deep place, and his art remains a tribute to the human spirit, appropriately revered by a persevering culture that adores poetry.

Man's Fate, by Andre Malraux, translated by Haakon M. Chevalier. (Review refers to the version in The Modern Library, New York, Random House; original copyright 1934 by Harrison Smith and Robert Haas, Inc.) Paralleling a growing recent interest in French poetry and existential philosophy/literature, I was attracted to this classic novel by adventurist/novelist Malraux. In the story of several intriguing characters of French, Chinese, Japanese and mixed background, it presents the failed Communist rebellion against the emerging power of Chiang Kai-shek and the Kuomintang in 1920's China. The nature and purpose of man are explored within the background of psychological factors related to colonialism (including their tragic residue as exuding from the often dismal foreign individuals remaining at its inevitable end), naïve hopes reflected in mass-held motivations toward radical changes, and fatalism of men and women caught in inescapable time and place, with the scattered flavorings of opium-derived wisdom. In this exotic tale, haunting lines, such as "One possesses of another person only what one changes in him," leap out viscerally far beyond their specific context and into the broader realm of universal human experience.

Science and the Akashic Field. An Integral Theory of Everything, by Ervin Laszlo. An easily readable account of some objective evidence for a true, and instantaneous, linkage of things in the universe: from the finally achievable postulated EPR experiment of Einstein (with perhaps different results than he'd expected) showing that past linked particles remain in shared symmetries over space (with "information" shared faster than the speed of light) in physics to proof for connection of individual consciousnesses. Many readers may already have faith in some such things, but as a scientist, seeing growing (and largely media ignored) strong objective data is a good aid to what I previously referred to as "killing the filter".

The God Theory. Universes, Zero-Point Fields, And What's Behind It All, by Bernard Haisch, Ph.D. This is a relatively brief, but interesting and enjoyable book, written by a renowned Astro Physicist. It is also easily approachable to non-scientists. Although his "theory" may not necessarily be new, per se (as elements are similar to ancient Vedantic or other prior philosophies about God), it is presented very nicely and with intelligent, well thought out incorporation of scientific discoveries, particularly from the realm of physics/astrophysics. It includes a reasonable attack on the fanaticism that the dogma of reductionist science has become in not keeping an open mind towards potentially spiritual matters. Haisch believes in God and our consciousnesses as a manifestation or extension of God because he FEELS it. He quotes widely from other Astro Physicists such as Sir Arthur Eddington and other great thinkers, such as the mescaline influenced Aldous Huxley. While primarily engaged in Astro and Solar Physics, Haisch briefly dabbled in complex mathematics addressing how electromagnetic fields in the quantum vacuum (or zero field) may be responsible for giving our energies mass effect and inertia. Whether to be substantiated and built upon further or not, related conclusions have phenomenal metaphysical implications regarding our interconnectedness and giving potentially staggeringly deep meaning to "The Light" of creation.

The Trial, by Franz Kafka, translated by Willa and Edwin Muir (Copyright 1937, Alfred A. Knopf, Inc., from the German *Der Prozess*, copyright 1925 by Verlag die Schmiede; copyright renewed 1974 by Schocken Books, Inc. Review refers to Definitive Edition, Schocken Books, New York, with additional material translated by E.M. Butler.) This book was a Christmas present from my son Travis. I had become interested in Kafka's take on what Camus called the "absurd". This brilliantly crafted and translated novel is a seemingly peculiar but wonderfully readable story of a regular working man (banker) charged with an uncertain offense, for which he can gain no solid information as to its nature or logical strategy for its defense. He becomes submerged in a mesmerizingly weird trip through a legal system that seems as if out of a bizarre dream that everyone understands but him. In a manner that justifiably earns cult-like status in one generation to the next, Kafka, through his posthumously published novel (the manuscript of which he had asked a close friend to burn after his death), exposes considerations that dwell somewhere very deep in the human psyche, finding the surface in such observations as "Logic is doubtless unshakable, but it cannot withstand a man who wants to go on living." Such penetrating thought tolls a bell that gets louder in my head each day. Clearly (even if the absurdists don't believe…), God places some tortured souls on Earth to help make us face the seemingly insurmountable challenges of being mortal humans, without which we could never start finding solutions.

Gulf Music, Poems by Robert Pinsky. Pinsky is a highly intelligent and provocative poet, who previously served as the Poet Laureate of the United States (1997-2000). I first encountered some of his poems including portions of "Essay on Psychiatrists" in an anthology of modern poetry, which prompted me to acquire a large collection of his prior writing, in addition to this recent collection published in 2007. The title may refer not only to the American Gulf Coast (evident in the content of some of the poems), the site of recent tragic disasters (even before the massive BP-related oil spill), but perhaps also to the gulf that we have collectively allowed to form between each of us as individuals (maybe even a poet of the people) living within the societies that we've formed. The poems frequently have an almost mysterious imagery with masterful application, and themes include the loss of memory and the meaning of things, to our detriment. The middle section explores what apparently simple objects around us mean in deep personal or abstract considerations, bringing the sense-perceived world to far more profound experience. In the mood for pondering, I enjoyed this collection and look forward to encountering more of his work.

The Birth and Death of Meaning, by Ernest Becker. (Review refers to *The Birth and Death of Meaning*, An Interdisciplinary Perspective on the Problem of Man, 2nd Edition, The Free Press, 1230 Avenue of the Americas, New York, NY 10020; copyright 1971.) Becker won a Pulitzer Prize for his prior book, *The Denial of Death*. Becker himself died of cancer at age 49. Even though *The Birth and Death of Meaning* was written in the early 1970s, its topics and arguments and conclusions are as relevant today as ever. This is simply one of the best non-fiction books I've ever read. The text is only 199 pages, but it is fairly densely packed with amazingly insightful observations, concepts, and thoughts. It is very readable, but it seems as if each sentence is informative and each page sparks light bulbs of awakened recognition and awareness. This is a brilliant analysis of the animal, social, and cultural reasons for why we act like we do – all of us, to each other, and how it may finally be feasible to alter these things to make a true open-minded humanism. If only I can hold to some of the most powerful conclusions expressed toward the end. For example, regarding true recognition of the despair imparted by our finitude and the non-solution of our "inner news-reels" and the current "hero-system" of our culture: "It is, as the Stoics and Shakespeare had already taught us, the going through hell of a lonely and racking rebirth where one throws off the lendings of culture, the costumes that fit us for life's roles, the masks and panoplies of our standardized heroisms, to stand alone and nude facing the howling elements as oneself – a trembling animal element...the banishment of one's self-respect to Hell; ... the disintegration of the self-esteem that sustains one's character." For me, this book was a revelation, and paralleled well some of the things I had read by R.D. Laing. I couldn't recommend this book enough.

The Precious Present, by Spencer Johnson. A Christmas present from Wayne and Katy Rigler. A short and nicely presented parable, the conclusion of which I won't spoil for anyone who has not yet read it, but might. I need to try to remind myself of this book's message every day, every moment, instead of agonizing over the latest neuronal death and each upcoming muscle loss and feeling sorry for myself.

News of the Universe. Poems of Twofold Consciousness, edited with introduction and comments by Robert Bly. A selection of well chosen poems (150 or so), with outstanding essays by Bly introducing the book and each of its six sections. This collection looks at man's changing relationship to Nature, as reflected in and sometimes led by poetry. It covers several centuries, from the "age of reason" (largely British poetry) in which man wanted to dominate (and hence ignore) nature; through German and French and other poets who began to see a consciousness in Nature and a oneness of man with Nature; through so-called object poems; through relevant works of some more modern poets; and concluding with mystical poems of Native Indians ("feather, not dot"), Eskimos, Indian ("dot, not feather") and other cultures, including poems by the likes of Kabir, Rumi, and Mirabai. The poetry journey helps lead to a perspective on Nature with which I've increasingly tried to view the physical (manifested) world.

The Inferno of Dante, translated by Robert Pinsky; illustrated by Michael Mazur. As noted, I became intrigued by Pinsky's poetry, and I also wanted to re-visit the horrific journey of Dante and Virgil through Hell. Perhaps I saw this as an allegory for what I wondered could be an emotionally survivable trip through my own darkness following an ALS diagnosis. So, I decided to read Pinsky's easily approachable translation (in terza rima form as the original Italian of Dante). Further, the monotypes by Mazur for each Canto are staggeringly powerful, prompting Travis and me to explore the artist's work further. The only problem is, Pinsky never translated *Purgatorio* or *Paradiso*, so now that I'm re-hooked after my first encounter nearly 30 years ago, I may have to go back to earlier translations.

The Stranger, by Albert Camus, translated by Matthew Ward. I'd clearly been in a "French mood" lately (who knew they did stuff besides wine...just kidding).

This concise, stylistically unusual classic novel is a fictional declaration of the issues of "the absurd" that Camus presented in the non-fiction analysis of *The Myth of Sisyphus*. Short, but for a slow reader like me to get through it in just two days while reading other books at the same time, it was obviously gripping. It may also go a bit towards explaining why I was in a bit of a black mood for a few subsequent days. We will all have to face the issue of our finiteness, as encompassed within the philosophy of Camus' "absurdity". Perhaps regarded by some as "existential", although I think the author may not have regarded his beliefs and works as such, it is a bizarrely enjoyable work, full of provocation despite the sparse prose (admirable to us long-winded types).

Noble Red Man. Lakota Wisdom Keeper Mathew King, compiled/edited by Harvey Arden. This was a present from Heidi's Aunt Marcia and Uncle Ave. As true Christians and intelligent humans, their spirituality allows for ideas held by those of other heritages, including Native American beliefs, such as those from the rich Lakota Sioux tradition. True and complete spiritual wisdom has deep connections in Nature's roots. This book is a wonderful compilation of wisdom sayings by King, a great spiritual leader of his people. Native Americans were far more connected to the powers and beauty of Nature than the greedy folks who came along and wiped them and much of their culture out.

The Essential Neruda. Selected Poems, edited by Mark Eisner (with translations from several contributors, in part to commemorate the 100th anniversary of Neruda's birth). THIS is what poetry at the highest levels can be! How fortunate I was to be able to read and experience some of this great man's works before this form passed. Even in (well crafted) English translations by a range of experts (with original Spanish on facing pages), these are among the most amazing works of poetry I've read. I'm jealous (but in an "innocent" kind of way) of those who can read them in Spanish. Now, Neruda ranks up there with Rilke as one of my favorite poets.

The Gospel of Thomas, translated and annotated by Stevan Davies. Thanks to Katy and some other friends for encouraging a visit here. Reading *The Gospel of Thomas* was fundamentally one of the most important processes in however far I've gone till now and however complete my spiritual journey may become. In this particular book, the included background sections were very informative and provided useful historic and religious perspective for the Gospel, and the annotations accompanying the sayings of Jesus provide some useful supplementation. This text likely existed before the canonical gospels were written, and the canonical gospels such as of Matthew and Luke appear to have borrowed from it. Sayings of Jesus are the sole content of this Gospel, most of which did not appear in the canonical Gospels included in the Bible, and the crucial messages of which are very different than those of the standard New Testament. This indeed is the very message I have sought all my life (and especially within the last year). Here we see that the Kingdom of Heaven is here and now (not something to transpire in some future time) and a wisdom of oneness that makes us all potentially the same as Jesus. There is no emphasis on original sin, no mention of crucifixion and resurrection; only a pure message of oneness and of finding the truth in this life, realizations that free man's spirit into the immortal Divine Consciousness. The Gospel of Thomas and the Vedas are hence of the same beautiful wisdom regarding our relationship to God and our connection to the Light of the beginning of the Universe, which we need to truly realize to be Divine. Divine love and power permeates everything.

The Stalin Epigram, by Robert Littell. This was a book I encountered thanks to my father-in-law Mike. It is an historic novel about the suppression of poetry (and just about all else....) during Stalinism told through the fate of the great poet Osip Mandelstam. The poet, perhaps unwisely but bravely and defiantly, wrote the fateful Epigram (poem about Stalin) in 1934, leading to his first arrest and exile. The story unfolds in alternating narratives from the various characters, including Mandelstam's wife Nadezhda, poet Anna Akhmatova, a Stalin bodyguard, and a former championship weight lifter (who shares a somewhat similar ridiculous arrest, torture, and punishment for having a suitcase with a picture of the Eifel Tower on it). This is a well written account by a veteran novelist of the personal suffering and collective endurance of suppression of thought, art, and life under oppressive conditions most of us could never imagine.

Eating the Honey of Words, New and Selected Poems, by Robert Bly. Having read some of Bly's poems in anthologies and in a collection he edited (referred to above), I became interested in pursuing a more in depth ingestion of his work. This is a wonderful collection of ~200 poems, presenting many poems from several of his previous books and ~10 new ones, covering nearly fifty years of Bly's poetry from 1950 – 1998. To me, at least, Bly is a masterful poet. His poems are particularly well crafted for reading out loud. They are often deceptively simple and direct, yet convey a complexity of emotions and sentiments. He is wise, but searching, expressing both an understanding and an ongoing longing for connection to nature and between human beings. He is real and vulnerable and his poems often celebrate humanity in the simplicity of daily life and through his recollections and regrets.

Krishna. The Supreme Personality of Godhead, Two Volumes, by A.C. Bhaktivedanta Swami Prabhupāda. This was a requested Christmas present, provided by Heidi. The current commemorative edition includes, as did the first edition, the introduction written by George Harrison, who funded the initial publication. The book represents the product of Swami Prabhupāda's study and translation of the Tenth Canto of *Śrīmad-Bhāgavatam*. It is a fascinatingly unique read on the life of Krishna (his transcendental pastimes) as support of Bhakti-Yoga. As far as this author is aware, in much of traditional or more conventional Hindu thought, Krishna is regarded as an avatar of the God Vishnu. As conveyed in the *Krishna* book, for the followers of Prabhupāda and Krishna devotees, quite simply, Krishna IS God (as the Supreme Personality of Godhead). Krishna is Brahman and can be known as a target of devotion. Hence, the stories of Krishna as presented by Prabhupāda in this book are to facilitate our knowing Krishna, and the attributes that Krishna demonstrates are those which we can love in God. Whether these related transcendental pastimes are to be regarded as true stories (e.g., in the same sense as the authors of the Bible Gospels intended for the miracles of Jesus) or as fantastic tales to facilitate love of God, it certainly makes for entertaining reading. No one kills monstrous demons, gets the girls, and conquers other armies (sometimes because of the girl....) better than the beautiful blue Krishna of Vrndāvana and Dvārakā. The interspersed spiritual explanations and teachings in Prabhupāda's translation are beautiful. Whether you regard Krishna as God or as an incarnation, if one keeps an open mind regarding cultural differences, this book is a wonderful tool in the practice of Bhakti-Yoga and God devotion.

Akhmatova Poems, translated by D.M. Thomas (Everyman's Library Pocket Poets series). Upon reading about the friendship of Mandelstam, Boris Pasternak, and Akhmatova in *The Stalin Epigram*, I wanted to read some of Anna Akhmatova's poetry. This is a fairly extensive collection from over her lifetime, with more than 100 poems included. About the same age as Mandelstam and popular with the Russian people (from her work in the 1910s, 1920s), she herself suffered under Stalin, who referred to her as "half nun, half harlot." Her first husband (poet Gumilev) was shot, her son was arrested multiple times, and best friends (like Mandelstam) were perpetually arrested, exiled, and killed. It's hard for us to imagine living under these circumstances, and I find in her work a powerful message of quiet courage and deep emotion and an inspirational wish for love, humanity, and the freedom to pursue art and life. Her poetry (before, during, and after the suppression) is poignant and honest, with a remarkably gentle sharing of personal experiences and feelings, including remorse.

Quantum Enigma. Physics Encounters Consciousness, by Bruce Rosenblum and Fred Kuttner. As with portions of the *Tao of Physics* (see above), this book predominantly deals with aspects of quantum physics that indicate the existence of observer-created reality. It then transitions to briefly consider the implications for human and cosmic consciousness. This book is presented in an easy reading format developed from a course taught by the authors. As expected, when physics gets to the seemingly "metaphysical" stage, many choose to ignore the "quantum enigma" and work in a practical manner in applying the discoveries of modern physics to such economic and societal mainstays as the many applications of laser, transistor, and semi-conductor technology. In an area where perhaps the boundaries of science and spirituality blur, the authors raise questions for which, of course, we don't yet have scientifically supported answers (and may never). They summarize various theories and approaches from those that aren't ignoring the "enigma," which make for some interesting thought.

Scientists and the Development of Nuclear Weapons. From Fission to the Limited Test Ban Treaty 1939-1963, by Lawrence Badash. I approached this book as someone who believes that pure science should be an objective search for truth and its applications rendered for universal help, but sadly recognizes that it must be conducted within the constraints and dangers of human-led societies. This book addresses a pivotal period in the evolution of the relationship of science to politics, war and economics. This is a well written, fairly brief book (part of *Control of Nature Series*; Humanity Books) that examines not only the role of scientists behind the technical aspects necessary for the development of atomic (nuclear) weapons, but also the new function of scientists in consequent political aspects in the nuclear age. This book provided fuel (maybe like manufactured plutonium isotopes) for thought on just what kind of world we little humans are making. I also learned a lot of historical and scientific details, including specific technologies in the Manhattan project, how the two bombs used in Japan differed, and the specific roles of some famous particle physicists.

Tarantula, by Bob Dylan. This is Dylan's only "novel", written in 1966. My father-in-law Mike gave it to me as a present, knowing that I may just be weird enough to read it I suppose. I slowly tackled this book, in part to transition from a perspective of a music fan to...something else. Although the necessary perspective may not be definable, the topic of the book could be loosely regarded as social psychology. The year and its corresponding period in American cultural history and in the complex evolution of Bob Dylan provide some clues to the content, commonly regarded as, at the very least, bizarre. Not really a novel in any conventional sense; it is more like a series of vignettes, written with one of the most unharnessed imaginations in the history of American or any other literature. This book is not for the casual Dylan fan or for someone looking for an introduction to Dylan. I cannot pretend that I understood all (or even most) of it, although that didn't stop me from enjoying the richly lyrical content. However, in the chapters (or portions of chapters) that I believed I gleaned some specific meaning from, there were absolutely brilliant, incredibly insightful, and amusingly clever commentaries on various issues facing society at that time (including the ludicrous role of hero-savior many were ascribing to Bob himself). Of course, many or all of these issues still face us today, often in even more frighteningly larger versions. Reality-checking art is always worth a visit.

Immortality, by Milan Kundera; translated by Peter Kussi. This is another highly intelligent novel by a gifted and well regarded writer. The clever prose conveys a thought provoking intermingling of characters in the present (including with scattered interactions involving the author himself, blurring the boundaries of reality and fiction with regard to the ongoing story) with literary and philosophical considerations presented in the context of past historical events. These involve tales from the personal life of the great German poet Goethe, who is also encountered in Heaven during interactions of past "immortal" artists Goethe and Hemingway, with a sprinkling of Rilke and others. The novelist's brilliant analyses of problems facing modern man and society are, as expected, insightful and yet refreshingly humorous. Few if any authors can impart so much "umph" about the human condition in such delicately intertwined narratives.

Crazy Diamond. Syd Barrett & the Dawn of Pink Floyd (New Revised Edition), by Mike Watkinson & Pete Anderson. This is the 2006 update of the biography originally published in 1991, to include additional information up to and following Syd's death in 2006. Having been a Pink Floyd fan since the advent of musical appreciation in high school, I'd read multiple books on the band. Of course, these include details about Syd Barrett as the songwriter, singer, and guitarist of the first version of Pink Floyd and his psychological demise, in the setting of extensive LSD use, essentially right after the release of the debut album *Piper At The Gates Of Dawn*. However, I wanted to learn more about the specifics of Syd's fate, including his post-Floyd largely reclusive life from the early 1970s on. I suppose part of my desire to encounter this topic again at this stage of my post-ALS diagnosis life was to further explore the potential attractiveness of a quiet and peaceful life under mental conditions that some might regard as "insane". As an extreme fan of the David Gilmour guitar driven Floyd, I also derived much more appreciation for the actual skill level and creativity of Syd Barrett, while being reminded of that long-established relationship between extreme creativity and psychotic tendencies and the fine line between genius and eventual insanity. I write this on the fourth anniversary of Syd's death, hoping along with millions of other fans, that this sensitive and brilliant artist eventually found peace (in this life, and especially the next one, to which we all make our journey at different paces... all the way up to "Interstellar Overdrive", I suppose).

A Brief History of Time. From the Big Bang to Black Holes, by Stephen W. Hawking, with introduction by Carl Sagan. In finally reading this book, which was published in the late 1980s, I was most interested in learning about theories on the origins of the universe, such as data supporting the Big Bang, as well as issues related to the fate of our universe. Hawking's contributions to these areas as well as the physics of Black Holes (always fun to read about) are, of course, impressive. I was hesitant to read this book after my diagnosis of ALS for personal reasons, reinforced by the cover picture of the exceedingly atrophic and crumpled author in his wheel chair. Yet, as I read, not only did I appreciate Hawking's ability to write of extraordinarily complex science in approachable language, but I was also pleased to see the frequent display of his sense of humor.

As many motor neuron disease patients realize, and hopefully this poet/scientist is increasingly appreciating, during the progressive loss of motor function, the mind seems to be capable of engaging in questions and thoughts that may not have even been ponderable before.

Hawking doesn't have "conventional" ALS. (At longer than 40 years survival post-diagnosis, he would be the longest survivor to date.) Hawking may have a particular variant of spinal muscular atrophy. Then again, at diagnosis, most of us "ALS" patients can't be certain that we're not affected by some other form of motor neuron disease. And we can't be certain how long we'll survive. But even if you didn't like any of the poems in this volume, trust the author when he says, "We're all going to die...at some point." (At least, this physical form will die.) This fading physician/scientist and fledgling poet/novelist is often more scared about how he is going to live with the progressive physical impairment of motor neuron disease...in that daily setting of increased challenges and growing constant reminder of what is happening. While reading this book, in addition to appreciating the great physical science and the skillful presentation, I found myself noting Dr. Hawking's courage and strength (YES, STRENGTH), which against all the other dark and scary moments, have shown in the light of his accomplishments during his career and important work. Whether I live 2 years, 5 years, 10 years, or more, it is this courage to carry on (and carry on well) despite the physical impairments that this scientist hopes he has also benefited from in the course of reading *A Brief History of Time*. And I look forward to reading *A Briefer History of Time* (the 2005 updated version by Stephen Hawking, with Leonard Mlodinow) and his new book as well.

Leaves of Grass. The First (1855) Edition, by Walt Whitman. (Review refers to version edited and with an introduction by Malcolm Cowley. Penguin Books, New York, New York. Copyright Viking Penguin Inc., 1959; Reprinted in Penguin Classics 1986.) This is obviously a classic. Yet, how fitting, I believe, to have come essentially full circle at this point from various books of poetry, Vedantic philosophy, and *The Gospel of Thomas* to this particular book-long poem with its related themes of the oneness of all things, including all souls. As pointed out in the excellent introduction by Cowley, the original 1855 version was likely prompted by the ecstatic vision (samadhi) that Whitman appeared to achieve in his own searching (including, apparently, so nature oriented). Based also on the revisions and additions in later versions (1856, 1860, up to the "deathbed" edition of 1881) paralleling what Cowley regards as subsequent "megalomania", "beatnik", and "good gray poet" phases in Whitman's life and career, the 1855 edition is the one that best conveys the message I have been seeking in other places as well. The poem contains many parallels to Vedantic philosophy and the teachings of Ramakrishna. This reinforced to me just how universal these ideas and realizations are, and how they can be appreciated anywhere: from the quiet of a meditation room to the wind blowing through a field of grass to a busy street or port filled with people. We and everything in this world, this universe, are all one. Whitman's own prose Introduction to the poem is long, and I read it only in short segments afterward. This work likely opened up new avenues in the use of free verse and the explorations of word and subject connections. It is an ecstatic proclamation of joy and spiritual recognition, with some pretty comforting words along the way. For example, from what would become the sixth chant of the section entitled "Song of Myself" (in later editions):

> *The smallest sprout shows there is really no death,*
> *And if ever there was it led forward life, and does not wait at the*
> > *end to arrest it,*
> *And ceased the moment life appeared.*
>
> *All goes onward and outward….and nothing collapses,*
> *And to die is different from what any one supposed, and luckier.*

And, I like that.

Peace
scotT

Notes

This section includes comments for some poems that had a particularly unique motivating factor or background. Also included are some explanatory notes for some terms or concepts from medicine and science or Hindu philosophy, which may not be broadly familiar.

First, a note on punctuation. In the introduction to the collection of Apollinaire poetry referred to in the Book List section of this volume, Roger Shattuck relates an interesting anecdote regarding the use (or lack thereof) of punctuation by the great French poet. When Apollinaire got the draft of his poetry book *Alcools* back from his editor, the punctuation had apparently been changed so much that he just decided to eliminate ALL of it. We perhaps erred to the opposite side of the spectrum. The incorporation of punctuation varies substantially in style in this current collection of poems, paralleling in part the dates that poems were written. Rather than striving for any sort of uniformity (a policy to which, in general, we are opposed), the punctuation stands for each poem as it was originally written...for better or worse...something that Katy Rigler refers to, maybe politely, as "part of the mystery of poetry."

Regarding use of punctuation in other portions of the book, the author notes that it may be "proper" to have all quotation marks outside end punctuation (as in sentence above). However, when quotes are used to indicate alternate meaning for, or a derogatory attitude toward, a word (as for "proper" in the sentence above), it doesn't make sense to put the quotation mark after a period simply as an artifactual coincidence that the quoted word fell at the end of the sentence; as if the whole sentence and not just the word were somehow "quoted." ... vs. "quoted". The former (.") may be in part a vestige of prior typeset and printing processes. As the poet has always struggled with things (like rules or social conventions) that are illogical, punctuation throughout the book adheres to a compromise or transition state, in which the old rules are followed when the content in quotation marks is an actual quotation, but for the other situations, a style is embraced which has been pleasantly referred to as "logical punctuation".

Darkness

The limbic system refers to a set of deep brain structures historically implicated in a variety of functions such as long term memory, behavior, and particularly emotions. Including the thalamus, hypothalamus, limbic cortex, and amygdala, the limbic system may have evolved prior to the neocortex so prominent in humans.

Interrogation of a Retrovirus

The retrovirus in the title refers to HIV, the causative infectious agent of AIDS. "Glands" is a common word used for the medically precise term lymph nodes. "Smart lab monkeys" refers to science researchers and technicians.

Ode to Ganesh

"Dark Horse" refers to George Harrison (whose lifelong spiritual journey involved a substantial Hindu and Krishna Consciousness component). Vedic refers to the Hindu philosophy of Vedanta (see Glossary). "Wisdom guide of writers" refers to Lord Ganesh, the object of the poem. Ganesh is one of Hinduism's most popular deities. Ganesh (or Ganesha) is the "Lord of obstacles", who helps smooth the way in human enterprises. He has an elephant head and a rather prominent belly. Ganesh is the lord of new beginnings and guardian of entrances. He has four arms that may hold a pasam, a goad, and a pot of rice or sweetmeats. He typically is depicted riding on a rat, an escort particularly well suited to gnawing through obstacles. Goads are symbolic of how one should steer the soul away from the ignorance and illusions of this earthly world, just as a "mahout" (the keeper and driver of an elephant) would steer an elephant away from any treacherous path. Ganesh's pot belly is usually bound around with a cobra, an animal associated with Shiva (his father). Ganesh's name literally means "Lord of Gana". He was entrusted with the leadership of the "ganas", Shiva's dwarfish and rowdy entourage. A pasam is a triple twine weapon. The three twines represent: arrogance and conceit; Maya, the illusory nature of the real world (see Glossary); and ignorance. This weapon is a symbolic tool to destroy the ego ("the clueless 'I'").

Ghosts of Ourselves Present

"Middledom" is a made up name to reflect a typical town or more likely, suburb, playing on the term middle class or being in the middle of typical daily life. "Quan" is a common Korean and less common Chinese family name. Quan Yin is a goddess of mercy in the Buddhist tradition. The word "Quan" or "Kwan" was used by the character Rob Tidwell (played by Cuba Gooding, Jr.) in Cameron Crowe's movie *Jerry Maguire* to reflect a personal state of harmony and well-being, similar to the meaning for its use herein.

Pearl Harbor Day in Big Bend National Park

Upon entering the park on December 7th, 2009 (during an RV trip), it was noted that the flag was hanging at half-mast. While staying at the RV during a hike by the others, the author wrote this poem. Javelina is the common name for the mammal also known as the collared peccary (*Tayassu tajacu*). They are protected in Big Bend National Park, where they are common. Adult animals can range from 3-4 feet long and weigh 45-85 lbs. They live in small herds of 5-20 animals. Predominantly herbivores and frugivores (fruit eaters), they will opportunistically eat meat. Typically avoiding human contact, they may be seen in campgrounds, including raiding unattended coolers and picnic tables. The prickly pear cactus represents approximately a dozen species of the *Opuntia* genus (Family *Cactaceae*). Varying in height from less than a foot to ~ 6 feet, they are found in all the deserts of the American Southwest, with several types present in Big Bend. In spring, they make beautiful flowers (yellow, red, purple) and in fall, cone-shaped fruits, most of which are edible.

On Reading Gide's "Immoralist"

In pondering some 17th-19th century English poetry, it appeared to the current author that to be a "typical" poet one has to write a poem or two about feelings experienced when reading works from some prior sage, perhaps celebrating the eternally enduring author. Upon reading André Gide's novel *The Immoralist*, the poet was moved to write one of these seemingly scholarly "while reading X's Y" kind of poems. As Keats (a truly immortal poet) had written poems on reading Homer and Shakespeare's *King Lear* and particularly because Keats himself died of tuberculosis (TB), the poet tried to tie this all together.

Brief summary of the novel: The powerful story magnificently accounted in *The Immoralist* takes place in the late 19th/early 20th century. It is a psychological exploration of the young Anthropologist Michel. He marries Marceline (whom he doesn't know) mainly to please his dying father. As they travel through Italy and Tunisia, Michel is suffering from TB, and as he begins to recover, he also starts to dislike his academic life, with its conservative French upper crust living, and begins to have "dark" feelings, including urges toward young Arab boys and then other men when back in France. The couple does conceive a baby, which is lost, as Marceline (with whom Michel does get along with very well) gets TB. In a perhaps metaphorical subconscious elimination from his life of things interfering with his newly awakening instincts, Michel takes Marceline on a long journey, intended consciously to heal her. Eventually, they arrive back in the Arab world, she dies and he has sort of bottomed out, despite the fact that he is now apparently living as a homosexual. It all begins with him telling this story in a somewhat confessional manner to some old friends that he has summoned to basically rescue him back home. It is not so much a defense of homosexuality (Gide was gay, and had an unconsummated marriage...), but a brilliant first person complex unfolding of man facing his "dark" side.

Bollingen is a village along the northern shore of Lake Zurich in Switzerland, were Carl Jung built his castle-like "Tower" over many years, in a form reflecting his knowledge of the structure of the psyche. For much of his later life he lived several months a year there, where he did much of his work.

La Bella Luna

Bella, half Chihuahua and half Beagle, is one of the dogs that belongs to friend Devette. LRD is the abbreviation for the poet's assigned nickname "little red Devette". The poet promised he would write a poem based on the caricature for Bella the group was creating one night as an extension of her real (typically impish) personality: a mysterious, previous countess, Mexican revolutionary, known to passionately sway the hearts and minds of citizens, as a cigarette casually dangles out of her mouth in charming cafes where revolutionaries tend to covertly gather.

Incurable Blues

"Despair upon despair" was a phrase noted by the poet when reading *Darkness Visible. A Memoir of Madness,* a personal account of depression by novelist William Styron (See Book List). The word terminal refers to nerve terminal, the part of the nerve cell that synapses on (connects to) another nerve cell. PEG tubes are percutaneous endoscopic gastrostomy tubes that are used for feeding directly into the stomach, as when swallowing may be impaired. The phrase "Do Not Go Gentle Into That Good Night" is from the Dylan Thomas poem title.

Passage

"Tat Tvam Asi" is a Sanskrit phrase translating to English such as "Thou Art That" or "That You Are". It implies that the "Self" is identifiable with the "Ultimate Reality". This awareness can only arise by direct realization or intuitive experience, not by inference from other (intellectual-type) knowledge.

Pessimism

The "dark poet of Providence" refers to American poet Edgar Allan Poe (1809-1849). Orpheus is a figure from Greek mythology serving as an important inspiration and subject in poetry, art, and literature. In classical Greece, Orpheus was held as the greatest poet and player of the lyre. One of the most famous stories of Orpheus is also the setting in which he is often tragically invoked in poetry. His new wife Eurydice was fatally bitten on her heal while walking in tall grass on their wedding day. Orpheus's song was so sad that the Gods advised him to visit the Underworld. His music softened Hades and Persephone, and they agreed to allow Eurydice to return with him to Earth, providing he walk in front of her and not look back until both had reached the upper world. As he reached the destination, however, he turned to see his adored bride, at which point she vanished again, but this time forever.

Present Awareness

This poem was written at the time of the poet's first Christmas following his ALS diagnosis. As he communicated to his sister, participation in the regular things (i.e., typical holiday time activities) can be a disturbing reminder of one's new condition and the treasured things that an ALS patient is inevitably going to miss out on (i.e., compared to a previously expected lifetime's worth). It is thus difficult to embrace such an occasion with the "normal" perspective. Instead, the poet reasoned that a more tolerable approach would be perhaps to become a bit "insane" to lessen the emotional pain. The phrase "tulip careless in the sick room" is a nod to (or a reference to) the Sylvia Plath poem *Tulips.*

"Where I come from..."

Bosons are a family of subatomic particles. These are often carriers of forces (such as photons in light). The phrase "rods and cones" refers to the photoreceptor cells of the retina.

To Serve

This poem was written for the author's sister, in support of a religious training experience called "Walk to Emmaus", which emphasizes service in the message of Christ (See Glossary). "Lust" and "greed" (or "woman" and "gold") are the English translations for the words that Sri Ramakrishna used to refer to the concepts of sexual and material desires that interfere with man's search for God.

Ode to Mom

This poem was written for the poet's mother (Alice Shappell) for her eightieth birthday (celebrated on December 27th, 2009 at Scott and Heidi's house). The phrase "two silver hearts" is a nod to the Shake Russell song "Two Silver Hearts". The future poet had arranged to have the Shake Russell Trio play at the surprise 50th anniversary party his sister and he had planned for their parents in New Braunfels, TX, October 15, 2008 (a few months before onset of symptoms of the poet's eventually diagnosed ALS). The song was played that night and dedicated to their parents Ralph and Alice.

I Reach Over

avīdyā – a term in Vedantic philosophy referring to ignorance, such as caused by the "real world" or Maya

Spring: From Lubbock to Colorado

This poem was written at the time of the graduation of the poet's son from college, one of the first "formal" outings of the author in a wheelchair. He rested in the hotel while most of the attending party went to the Buddy Holly Museum for the day. The poet then went on to spend several weeks with his sister Sally and his brother-in-law Kel at their remote property outside Pueblo, CO (with wondrous views of the Wet Mountains). The phrase "viewers and shapers" is a reference to pathologists (profession of poet's wife and the poet; who, of course, look through microscopes) and architects (field of study of the poet's son, subsequently continuing in graduate school), respectively.

Ouch and Love

The idea of attempting a unique structural framework in a poem was inspired in part by the poetry of Guillaume Apollinaire (See Book List). The author of the current collection decided he would write a "syllabic-delineated" poem, in which he would start with a stanza of lines of 1, 2, 3, 4, 5, 6, 7, 8, 9, and 10 syllables, then proceed with stanzas with lines of 2, 3, 4, 5, 6, 7, 8, 9, 10, ...3,

4, 5...etc. syllables, and then descend from 10, 9, 8, 7, 6, 5, 4, 3, 2, 1 in one final stanza to reach a conclusion. Regarding the word kundalini, see definition in Notes to *Outsiders Heading to the Grass* below.

Perspective

This poem was written at night, immediately after the holiday party for the author's laboratory (end of first year of his ALS). Related comments are included in a correspondence within the Spiritual Correspondences section.

Outsiders Heading To The Grass

kundalini – In Hindu yoga, the term kundalini literally means "the Serpent Power". It refers to the spiritual energy that is dormant in all individuals. According to the Tantra (see Glossary), there are six dynamic centers (chakras) in the body. In these mystical centers, the spiritual energy becomes vitalized and finds special expression with appropriate spiritual perception and mystic vision. These centers are localized within the "nervous system" and in the path to realization, they form the ascending steps by which the kundalini or spiritual energy passes from the base of the spine to the cerebrum.

squamous mucosa – refers to the histological type of epithelium (surface cells) lining the esophagus (as well as oral cavity)

cingulate – refers to the cingulate cortex part of the brain (or the cingulate gyrus, part of the cingulate cortex), along the medial (inner) aspect of the cerebral cortex; an integral part of the so-called limbic system, involved in emotions and memories

neo-cortex – refers to the outer most layer of the cerebral hemispheres, regarded as the latest evolving (newest) part of the human brain; involved in higher functions of motor commands, sensory perception, language, and thought

nephrons – the functioning units of the kidney

occipital – refers to the occipital lobe of the brain, posteriorly located and involved in visual perception

Vedantic – see Glossary

Broca – Paul Broca was a 19th century French neuroanatomist and physician best known for discovering the link of speech production to a specific region of the brain. By studying symptoms of patients and correlating with autopsy findings, he deduced that patients with lesions (damage) in a certain region of the left inferior frontal lobe of the brain had an expressive aphasia (a speech impairment characterized by difficulty in articulating words). This became known as Broca's aphasia and the implicated region of the brain designated as Broca's area.

sheath – refers to the physical and temporary body, a term characteristically employed by Sri Ramakrishna, and in contrast to the immortal soul.

"Outsiders" in the title is in part a reference to the term employed by Colin Wilson (in the late 1950s-1960s) to refer to that very small minority of humans who cannot adjust in a "sane" fashion to the "insanity" of modern society and who see things differently, perhaps based on a truer grasp of cosmic and human reality. "Heading to the Grass" is a nod to the beautiful work of Pink Floyd regarding insanity (a major theme of the albums *The Dark Side of the Moon, Wish You Were Here,* and *The Wall*), particularly the lyrics in *Brain Damage* at the end of *The Dark Side of the Moon.*

Cruel Teacher

The masterful poet, Charles Baudelaire, transformed the content of verse and ushered in the hope of wholeness through awareness by his celebrations of the darker elements of society, as in *Les Fleurs du Mal.* With much effectiveness, his poems, such as "Reversibility", occasionally included repeat of lines at the beginning and end of stanzas. Recognizing the huge gap between what this diseased poet/scientist is capable of expressing compared to the essentially sacred contributions of Baudelaire, the style of this poem is in part an acknowledgement to those things the author hopes he has gained from the art of Baudelaire and other wise souls.

Sisyphean – refers to Sisyphus. In Greek and Roman mythology, Sisyphus was a king who was punished by the gods for his trickery and belief that his cleverness surpassed that of Zeus. He was forced to roll a huge bolder up a hill, only to watch it roll back down, and to repeat this throughout all eternity.

Glossary

ashram – a religious hermitage (typically remotely located) where residents may undergo religious instruction and perform spiritual exercises

Atman – the Self or Soul; in Advaita Vedanta philosophy, the Supreme Soul, which is one with the individual soul

Bhakti-Yoga – the spiritual path of devotion and love of God; can include worship of a chosen deity or prophet as object of devotion

Brahman – the Absolute, which cannot be comprehended; the Supreme Reality of Vedanta philosophy

brāhmin – a member of the priestly caste (highest caste in Hindu society)

Brāhmo Samāj – a Hindu reform organization established in 19th century India; conflict regarding incorporation of ideas from Christianity resulted in subsequent schisms and formation of other organizations

butte – (included for us flatlanders) an isolated hill or mountain with steep sides and a smaller summit area than a mesa

dualist – an adherent of the dualistic philosophy of Vedanta, in which the embodied individual soul is different from God, and for whom there is separation between consciousness and matter (see also non-dualist)

"Existence-Knowledge-Bliss Absolute" – see Satchidānanda

ISKCON (International Society of Krishna Consciousness) – a religious organization founded by A.C. Bhaktivedanta Swami Prabhupāda in New York City in 1966; known as the Hare Krishna movement, it centers on Bhakti-Yoga, with its devotees dedicated to serving and worshiping Krishna as God

japa – repetition or chanting of God's name or mantra

Jnana-Yoga – the spiritual path of knowledge, in which realization of the Self is arrived at through reasoning, renunciation, and discrimination; leads to the awareness of one's identity with the Absolute (realization of the oneness of the Atman with Brahman, a truly mystical state)

Jung – the Swiss psychiatrist Carl Gustav Jung (1875-1961); although a practicing psychiatrist and a pioneer of analytical psychology and dream analysis, Jung regarded the human psyche as by nature religious; known for such concepts as the process of individuation, Archetypes, and the Collective Unconsciousness

Kāli (Mother Kāli) – a name for the Divine Mother (in Hinduism); represents the Primal Energy; the presiding Deity of the Dakshineswar temple, where Sri Ramakrishna spent his adult life

Karma-Yoga – the spiritual path of deeds and service, by which the aspirant seeks to realize God through unselfish work

Math – a Hindu monastery

Maya – in Vedantic philosophy, a term referring to the cosmic illusion by which the One appears as many (i.e., separate people, separate things) and by which the Absolute appears as relative; in essence, what we consider the real world of our daily lives

non-dualist – an adherent of the non-dualistic philosophy of Vedanta (such as in the Advaita school), in which everything is regarded as Brahman and no distinction is seen between consciousness and matter; a believer in the unity of the Atman (Self) with Brahman (the Absolute) (see also dualist)

prema – ecstatic love for God of the most intense kind

Raja-Yoga – the spiritual path of concentration (including discipline in meditation), to eventually achieve liberation

samadhi (Samadhi) – ecstasy (as in a trance) when in communion with God

sannyasin – a wandering (Hindu) monk and/or one who has renounced all attachments; sannyas is the monastic life, which is the last of the four stages of life in traditional Hindu philosophy (see also vanaprastha)

Satchidānanda – sanskrit term, translating to Existence-Knowledge Bliss Absolute; hence, referring to Brahman, the Ultimate Reality

Śrīmad-Bhāgavatam – an ancient Hindu text, with a primary focus of Bhakti and incarnations of Vishnu, particularly Krishna

Stephen Ministry – a not-for-profit religious educational organization designed to help Church congregations train members to be Christ-centered caregivers for the needy within their community; founded in 1975 and based in St. Louis, MO (www.stephenministries.org)

Tantra – a system of religious philosophy (and its scriptures) in which the Divine Mother is the Ultimate Reality; takes into account the natural weakness of human beings and their lower appetites, incorporating rituals, ceremonies, and material enjoyment

Upanishads – the last and latest written portions of the sacred Vedas (see below), forming the basis for Vedantic non-dualist philosophy (essentially identical to the Advaita system); meaning of the word Upanishad in Sanskrit is complex and may include in part "sitting near" and "annihilating ignorance"; convey the wisdom by which the individual soul or Atman realizes its oneness with Brahman, the Absolute and Supreme Reality

Vaishnava – a Hindu Bhakti sect (or member of sect) devoted to the God Vishnu and stressing image worship

vanaprastha – the third stage of life in traditional Vedic philosophy, which is the forest dweller or hermit stage; typically reached at age 50, when the individual retreats from the world (and working life) and concentrates on spiritual matters (see also sannyasin)

Vedanta – literally, the ends or concluding parts of the Vedas; a system of philosophy elaborated primarily in the *Upanishads*, the *Bhagavad Gītā*, and the *Brahma Sutras*; followers may be dualist or non-dualist (see glossary entries)

Vedas – the most sacred scriptures of Hinduism, the authority of which is accepted by all orthodox Hindus

Vishnu – the Supreme God in the Vaishnava tradition; in the trimurti ("three forms") concept of Hinduism, regarded as the God who maintains the universe (along with Brahma the creator, and Shiva the destroyer)

viveka – discrimination in Vedantic philosophy; the ability, as a consequence of continuous intellectual effort, to distinguish between the real and the unreal, the permanent and the temporary, and the Self and not-Self

"Walk to Emmaus" – an ecumenical spiritual training program sponsored through local groups by The Upper Room, a ministry unit of The United Methodist Church; begins with a 72-hr course, which includes small group sessions; in the Bible, Emmaus was town where Jesus appeared to a small number of his disciples following his resurrection

Wilburys (Traveling Wilburys) – the "supergroup" composed of George Harrison, Bob Dylan, Roy Orbison, Jeff Lynne, and Tom Petty; the Wilburys made two albums (the second without Roy Orbison, who had passed away), but called them Volume One and Volume Three, respectively

About the Author and Contributors

Dr. Scott B. Shappell was born as a U.S. military dependent in Heidelberg, Germany, on November 11, 1962. He graduated from the University of Dallas with a B.S. in Physics, Magna Cum Laude in 1984. Attending Baylor College of Medicine, Houston, TX, he earned his M.D., with High Honors, and his Ph.D. in Pharmacology in 1991. He completed residency training in Anatomic Pathology and a fellowship in Renal Pathology at Baylor College of Medicine Affiliated Hospitals from 1992-1996. He served on the faculty in Pathology, Urology, and the Vanderbilt-Ingram Cancer Center from 1997-2003 at Vanderbilt University Medical Center, Nashville, TN. Recipient of multiple federal grants for prostate research and a co-investigator on an additional ten grants focused on prostate carcinoma, Dr. Shappell has authored more than 60 peer-reviewed original biomedical research articles and another ~20 text book chapters, case reports, and review articles. From 2004-2007, he served as Director of Molecular Pathology, Director of Research, and Medical Director for Reference Laboratories in Nashville, TN and Dallas, TX. In July 2007, with two partners from Mattison Pathology Lubbock, TX, Dr. Shappell established a laboratory in Dallas as part of Avero Diagnostics, a broadly focused surgical and molecular pathology laboratory, with substantial effort in translational research.

Dr. Shappell has been married to Dr. Heidi W. Shappell since 1998, and has one son Travis, currently a graduate student in architecture at Texas Tech University in Lubbock, TX. Following his diagnosis of ALS in April 2009, Dr. Shappell has focused more time on non-research writing. This is his first published volume of poetry.

Sally F. Kilpatrick was born Sally Frances Shappell in Dayton, KY, in 1959. She attended the University of Texas, San Antonio, graduating with a B.A. degree in English in 1981, with a particular interest in the American Gothic Novel. Various accounting department jobs and partial life stories led her to work in San Antonio, TX, Columbia, SC, and Houston, TX, where she acquired a career with the Internal Revenue Service, a husband named Kelsal, and two step-children. She was a member of the Presbyterian Church in The Woodlands, TX, and she and Kel are currently members of the First Presbyterian Church of Pueblo, CO. They live outside of Pueblo on 50 acres, complete with their own butte. A prior Church Elder, Sally is currently a Stephen's Minister. She is a lifetime passionate reader of varied prose literature and poetry, with favorite poets including Walt Whitman, Robert Frost, and William Blake.

Katherine Jeannine Lauer Rigler was born in Pampa, TX in 1973 and grew up in Nashville, TN. She received a B.S. degree from the University of Tennessee at Chattanooga and worked as a licensed physical therapist for several years before answering a call to the ministry. In 2003 Katy graduated Magna Cum Laude from Vanderbilt University with a Masters in Divinity. While pursuing a PhD in Religion at Vanderbilt, focusing in Homiletics and Liturgics, she developed severe and ongoing calcium homeostasis complications following routine thyroid surgery in April 2007. After a second Masters in Religion, Katy has devoted the last three years to regaining her health, caring for her family, teaching and preaching. Her health issues significantly improved after beginning a mostly raw vegan diet. She writes about her lifestyle as a raw vegan, the home schooling of her children, and spiritual issues on her blog at http://katy-uncooked.blogspot. com. Katy has had a life-long love of poetry and literature. Some of her favorite poets include Rumi, Hafiz, Wendell Berry, Marge Piercy, and Sylvia Plath. An ordained Presbyterian minister, Katy lives in Plano, TX, with her husband Wayne and their three children Jake, Emma and Phillip.

Dr. Simon Hayward is currently an Associate Professor in the Departments of Urologic Surgery and Cancer Biology at Vanderbilt University Medical Center, Nashville, TN. He is an internationally recognized prostate expert, with research interests in prostate development, benign prostatic hyperplasia (BPH), and prostate carcinoma. Dr. Hayward earned his B.S. degree with Honors at Westfield College (University of London), an M.S. degree at Birkbeck College (University of London), and his Ph.D. in 1991 at the Imperial Cancer Research Fund (now Cancer Research, U.K.) He completed a Postdoctoral Fellowship at the University of California, San Francisco, where he remained as a researching faculty member from 1995 until 2001, when he joined the faculty at Vanderbilt University. A past and current recipient of multiple NIH and Department of Defense prostate research grants and a co-investigator on numerous other grants, Dr. Hayward has authored more than 80 peer-reviewed original research articles and more than 40 text book chapters and review articles. Because of his expertise in unique approaches to prostate tissue models, dozens of investigators from other laboratories have visited the Hayward Lab for training. He has served on the American Urological Association's Research, Education, and Meeting Planning Committees and has been an officer in the Society of Basic Urologic Research for more than a decade, including President in 2009-2010.

Dr. M. Scott Lucia is currently an Associate Professor of Pathology, Chief of Genitourinary and Renal Pathology, and Director of the Prostate Diagnostic Laboratory at the University of Colorado Health Sciences Center (UCHSC), Denver, CO. He was born in Colorado Springs, CO in 1961 and graduated Magna Cum Laude from the University of Denver in 1984. He earned his M.D. with honors from the University of Colorado School of Medicine, in Denver in 1988 and completed residency training in Anatomic and Clinical Pathology at UCHSC, Denver, CO from 1988 to 1993. He continued his training as a Research Fellow in the Laboratory of Chemoprevention at the National Cancer Institute, Bethesda, MD from 1993-1995, before returning to join the faculty at UCHSC. Dr. Lucia is a nationally known expert in prostate pathology and prostate research, including in support of large multi-center clinical trials. Recipient of numerous federal and private research grants and a collaborator on many others, Dr. Lucia is the author of 80 peer reviewed research manuscripts and 20 additional reviews and text book chapters. He is also a highly regarded teacher, having served as the Director of the Pathology Residency Program and having received numerous teaching awards from the medical students at UCHSC. In addition to his professional accomplishments, Dr. Lucia has been involved in numerous community youth programs and has been the pianist at the New Hope Presbyterian Church in Castle Rock, CO since 2003.

Dr. Stanley Appel is the Peggy and Gary Edwards Distinguished Endowed Chair for the Treatment and Research of ALS, Department of Neurology, The Methodist Hospital; Senior Member, The Methodist Hospital Research Institute; Director, Methodist Neurological Institute; Houston, TX and Professor of Neurology, Weill Cornell Medical College of Cornell University. Dr. Appel received his B.A. degree from Harvard University and his M.D. from Columbia College of Physicians and Surgeons. He completed his internship in Internal Medicine at the Massachusetts General Hospital, Boston, MA, before undergoing his residency training in Neurology at Mount Sinai Hospital, New York, NY. He previously served as Chief of Neurology and the James B. Duke Professor of Medicine at Duke University Medical Center, NC, and as Chair of the Department of Neurology at Baylor College of Medicine, Houston, TX. Dr. Appel is an internationally recognized expert in the treatment and research of ALS. In 1982, he created what is now the Methodist Neurological Institute's MDA/ALS Research and Clinical Center in Houston, the first multi-disciplinary clinic in the U.S. dedicated to care and research for ALS patients. Over his distinguished career that has spanned more than 40 years, Dr. Appel has authored 15 books and over 350 articles on topics such as ALS, neuromuscular disease, Alzheimer's disease, and Parkinson 's disease. He is a Fellow of the American Association for the Advancement of Science and his numerous awards include the Sheila Essey Award in 2003 from the American Academy of Neurology for "outstanding research in Amyotrophic Lateral Sclerosis", the MDA's Wings Over Wall Street Diamond Award in 2004, and the Forbes Norris Award for "compassion and love for humanity in research and treatment in patients with ALS" from the International Alliance of ALS/MND Associations in 2005. He has trained more than 200 neurologists and has treated more than 3,000 ALS patients, more than any other physician in the U.S.

LaVergne, TN USA
15 February 2011
216699LV00004B/5/P